The Jewish-Japanese Sex and Cook Book and How to Raise Wolves

Books by Jack Douglas

Benedict Arnold Slept Here: Jack Douglas' Honeymoon
        Mountain Inn
A Funny Thing Happened to Me on My Way to the Grave
The Jewish-Japanese Sex and Cook Book and How to Raise Wolves
Shut Up and Eat Your Snowshoes!

JACK DOUGLAS

*The Jewish-Japanese
Sex and Cook Book
and
How to Raise Wolves*

THE JEWISH-JAPANESE SEX AND COOK BOOK
AND HOW TO RAISE WOLVES

ISBN-13: 978-1535328197
ISBN-10:1535328193

PRINTING HISTORY
Putnam edition published 1972

*To my lovely family
and Flents Ear Stopples*

The Jewish-Japanese
Sex and Cook Book
and
How to Raise Wolves

1

"SPEAKING of whores," Harry Mitchell said, looking across his deep-dish martini to some far distant horizon, "I remember once in Butte, Montana, this whore had a dog—" Then he lapsed into what seemed to be some form of catatonia.

"That *all* there *is* to the story, Harry?" Ruthie Mitchell, Harry's semilovely wife, said after a long pause.

"Huh?" Harry said.

"Anybody wanna tea?" Reiko asked, always the perfect hostess.

"Nobody's drinking tea, Reiko dear," I said with Clint Eastwood suavity.

"What kind of a dog?" Harry said, swallowing a hiccup along with his stuffed olive.

"What?" Ruthie said.

"What kind of a dog did this whore in Butte, Montana, have?"

"How the hell would *we* know?" I said. "It's *your* story."

"Oh," Harry said, then to Reiko, "Did you put vodka in this vodka martini?"

"Yes," Reiko said.

"Well, no wonder," Harry said, "no wonder I'm getting pissed."

"Yeah, that'll do it, Harry," Ruthie agreed. "I read it in *Time* magazine. It was the cover story on June 16, 1959."

"It was a St. Bernard," Harry said.

"What was?" Reiko wanted to know, even though she didn't really understand any of it.

"The dog that whore in Butte, Montana, had," Harry said. "A St. Bernard."

"That's a very good story," I said. "Harry, you *sure* can *tell* 'em."

"It's not the end of the story," Harry said. Archly.

"It isn't?" Ruthie wanted to know. Harry ignored his semi-lovely wife and turned to me, sloshing his everfilled martini glass over his red suede vest.

"Have you ever had a St. Bernard watch you hump?" he said.

"Well," I said, "I've always liked dogs, but—"

"Of course you haven't," Harry said. "This St. Bernard stood right on that Butte, Montana, whore's bed, and when it was all over he lifted his leg—on *me*."

There was an exceptionally quiet silence after this. No one knew exactly what to say. I, for one, felt that "Congratulations" might be inappropriate. Or inadequate.

This enlightening and little-known incident in Montana's exciting history, as relayed by that superb storyteller Harry Mitchell, was told as part of an ecology lecture which Harry Mitchell had promised to give at the first meeting of the Honansville Ecology Group—a new organization, which was formed by concerned, ecology-minded citizens of Honansville who liked to drink.

This was the way it looked to me, but I felt that some good might come of these well-intentioned, if somewhat unsteady, people. Wolf, our wolf, was almost a year old; and I had joined several groups that were trying to save the wolves and the many other endangered species because, I think, the closer I got to know the wolf through my everyday association with this unique animal, and from reading and discovering the definite need we have for *every* animal left on earth, they all seemed to be part of a pattern or plan that, if altered much more, could destroy us. The great chain of nature, of which *every* living thing is a part, must not be broken. I had learned very rapidly how important it is that something needs doing *now!*

When I looked around our living room on this first meeting night of the Honansville Ecology Group, I wondered if I had chosen the right course.

We were a smallish group. There was Frank Krasselt, an artist with a tremendous old red barn in back of his

1772 Connecticut saltbox house stacked to the hayloft with his unsold paintings of 1772 Connecticut covered bridges. His wife, Ethel Krasselt, also painted and had to rent an old red barn to store *her* vast collection of unsold paintings. She painted tiny, doll-like little girls with enormous wide-open blue eyes which were supposed to haunt you (into buying a painting, I presume). Ethel Krasselt, as a sideline, had a red-hot kiln in which she baked fake American Indian pots which were sold for genuine at the local Indian pot shop, which also sold gas, rock candy, maple sugar, and "farm fresh" eggs which they bought from the A & P. Frank and Ethel's ecology crusade was directed at eliminating one Mr. Ernie Saloks, the local gravel pit king and chief land destroyer. Ernie Saloks' present project was the taking of gravel from the roadside gravel mine and dumping the residue into a nearby swamp, thus endangering the red-winged blackbird, so reported Frank and Ethel Krasselt.

"There won't be a cattail left!" wailed Ethel Krasselt.

"What's a cattail?" Reiko wanted to know.

"That's what the red-winged blackbirds sit on," Frank Krasselt said.

Reiko didn't say anything.

Virgil Palmquist and Reggie Mailer, who were the proprietors of the Yellow Prune, a local antique shop, and who went roaming through the gloaming when the weather was nice, hand in hand, also graced (and I think this is just the right word) our living room.

Virgil and Reggie were very ecologically concerned with the gray squirrel.

"Our gray squirrel," Virgil said, "is becoming a nervous wreck! I'm sure that any day now he's just going to go to pieces, and then what will we do? Who can you turn to with a nutty squirrel?"

"Yeah," I sympathized, "not many psychiatrists specializing in squirrel problems."

"Oh, *you!* Reggie said, twitchingly. *"You* don't think it's serious! You should just be there once and see what that lousy little red squirrel does to our big gray squir-

11

rel! It's embarrassing!" Harry Mitchell's deep and lasting interest in his drink was dissipated by this.

"You mean to say," Harry Mitchell said, "a little red squirrel is balling a big gray squirrel? Unbelievable! Utterly unbelievable!"

"We'd better call the Audubon Society the first thing in the morning," Ruthie Mitchell said.

"We'd better call 'em right *now!*" Harry said, making a lurch toward our phone.

"Wait a minute," I said.

"It's nothing like *that!*" Virgil screamed like Maria Callas at La Scala. "Nothing like that! It's just that the lousy little red squirrel keeps chasing our big gray squirrel away from the nut box!"

"What nut box?" I asked—timidly, I must admit.

"The box where we keep the nuts for our gray squirrel to eat—but he can't eat them because the red squirrel keeps chasing him away and then the red squirrel stuffs himself silly! What's ecology going to do about *that????*"

All of us, including Bobby and Timothy, had a drink after this to steady *our* nerves and to ponder a bit. After a two-minute ponder, Bobby said, "I *like* red squirrels."

"You would!" Virgil, trying to fork his tongue, said to Bobby, "I'll bet you like hockey, too—dontcha?" Before Bobby could answer, Bella Brown, who was built and looked more than a little like Rocky Graziano, and who had taken over Women's Lib in northwestern Connecticut, said to Virgil and Reggie, "Gentlemen, that is the law of the survival of the fittest."

"Christ!" Virgil muttered to Reggie, indicating Bella. "If that's a law—*she's* gonna survive *all* of us!"

Bella continued, after rolling up her sleeves to reveal biceps like that golden man holding something up (or whatever he's doing) at Rockefeller Plaza. Bella wasn't displaying her physical superiority to everything that breathed in Honansville, she was just sweating a little after six boilermakers. "Gentlemen, the red squirrel isn't afraid of anything. So if you're smart, let him have the nuts."

Mr. and Mrs. Rogers Dotson completed our little ecology group. Mr. and Mrs. Rogers Dotson-joined *every-thing* that was against *anything*.

Alice Dotson was out of the dowager mold and was bosomy to the point of being mountainous. Rogers Dotson smoked a sulfurous meerschaum pipe and sat in our most comfortable easy chair, stroking the air with his left hand. Stroking and caressing.

"What the hell is *that?*" I whispered to Harry Mitchell.

"It's nothing," Harry Mitchell said. "He's so used to sitting in front of his own cozy fireplace all day long and petting his favorite Irish setter that when he goes out he can't kick the habit—somehow, he thinks the dog is there with him and needs stroking."

"Oh," I said.

"Yeah," Harry Mitchell said, "a coupla years ago when he first started to do it, I thought he had horizontal palsy."

The Honansville Ecology Group was meeting in our living room because we were the ones who owned a wolf so, as someone had said when the idea for an ecology group was in its formative stage, I was the one who stood to gain the most from the preservation of our natural resources. I didn't quite understand how, but I didn't fight it. This is the reason the first meeting of the Honansville Ecology Group met at *our* house, and because everyone else had good reason not to have any gathering at *their* houses. Frank and Ethel Krasselt's living room was also their studio and too cluttered with easels, paint, and great gobs of clay with which Ethel made her pots, so there was really no room, they said, to hold any kind of meeting. Virgil and Reggie said their antique shop was no place for careless drinkers; and besides, when business hours were over and they closed the drapes, lighted the incense and the candles, and put a stack of Bessie Smith LP's on their record player, they had had it for the day, and any intrusion into this epicene paradise would be a sacrilege.

Bella Brown's excuse for not having any meetings at her place was more direct. Her living room, which was housed in a not-quite converted stable, was also used by her to shoe her horses, and she'd be goddamned if she was going to move her goddamned anvil out just to let a lot of nonhorses in.

Mr. and Mrs. Rogers Dotson said they couldn't have meetings at their place because it would be un-American. When some brave soul asked what the hell this meant, Mr. Dotson, whom I remembered as having a thing for Norfolk jackets, said, "Please don't question my judgment. Ask me anything you wish, but please—*please* don't question my judgment!" Well, this left us exactly nowhere, but we *didn't* question Mr. Dotson's judgment. He and his wife were really quadruple threats—they were bigots, conservatives, liberals, and reactionaries. This left them very little time to go to the bathroom. And the Dotsons didn't help very much with our grandiose plans for protecting the environment. But we all felt they might be inveigled by some fast double-talk to part with some of their vast fortune (and it *was* vast) if they felt they could play some small part in stamping out civilization. So long as it didn't include them and their cosy little forty-acre estate with its manor house, its heated duck pond, and its seventeen-car garage.

This splendid example of the democratic way left the whole thing up to *us*. Either we met at our house or in an open field somewhere. There were very few open fields left around Honansville open to an ecology group. Most of the farmers were suspicious of anyone who didn't shoot crows, foxes, woodchucks, and other "varmints" and who believed in getting rid of garbage in some other way than heaving it in the "crick" or burning it for days in a smoldering, smoky, rat-colonied dump.

"I think we ought to have a potluck supper," Virgil Palmquist said.

"Good idea," Reggie Mailer agreed.

"What the hell has a potluck supper got to do with pollution?" Harry Micthell said.

"That's what I'd like to know," Bella Brown said, biting off a huge chunk of her endless supply of chewing tobacco with all the finesse of a tiger shark attacking a

14

weight watchers' swimming party. Reiko, always thoughtful, promptly placed a bucket next to Bella.

"You're very thoughtful," Bella said.

"I repeat," Harry Mitchell said, stirring his fifth martini with his soggy index finger, "what the hell has a potluck supper got to do with pollution?!"

"Well, for one thing," Virgil said, almost stamping his dainty baby-pink loafer, "have you ever *been* to a potluck supper? There's *nothing* more polluted!"

"Oh, a joke," Harry Mitchell said. "Very funny."

"With a potluck supper," Reggie Mailer lisped, menacingly, coming to the defense of his muliebrous partner, "we could raise some money for the cause."

"The *cause?*" Rogers Dotson's eyebrows shot up in the direction of his 1928 hairdo. "Sounds a little pinko to me, Buddy!"

"Oh, *you* know what I mean," Reggie said, pinching Rogers Dotson's tweed knee. "Now don't you? Admit it!"

"I don't think the Indians are getting a fair shake," Ethel Krasselt, the Indian pot counterfeiter, said. "Look at the Mocadoc Reservation." She waved her nondrinking hand in the direction, more or less, of the Mocadoc Reservation, which was upriver a bit from Honansville.

"Yeah," Bella Brown said, "most of the Indians up there are niggers."

"Then they can't be Indians," Virgil Palmquist said, dismissing the whole subject with a flick of his swiveled wrist.

"Oh, *no!?*" Bella said, rather belligerently. "Look, Buster, in America a nigger can be any goddamn thing he goddamn wants to be. Put that in your goddamn pipe and smoke it!"

"I'll buy a pipe first thing in the morning," Virgil said, "and for your information"—he was getting imperial now —"niggers aren't called niggers anymore—they're called blacks." Bella aimed a Niagara of tobacco juice at the pail Reiko had so thoughtfully provided and let it go. It missed the pail completely. Reiko had guessed wrong on the trajectory and the wind drift.

15

"Speaking of whores—" Harry Mitchell said.

"Anybody wanna tea?" Reiko asked, hoping that Bella might give up Mail Pouch for Tetley's while we still had some virgin carpeting left.

2

EVERY morning, rain or shine, sleet or snow, hail or showers of little green men (and women), I used to take my wolf, whose name was Wolf, for a long walk through the hills of northwestern Connecticut, where we were domiciled, temporarily, I hoped, after deserting our forest home in Canada.

Walking Wolf was not really a daily pleasure that I looked forward to with great and happy anticipation. There were times when it was a big bucolic bore. I didn't give a damn how beautiful the Connecticut hills were. Hills were hills. Then there were other times when the whole project seemed to get out of hand. What started as a peaceful stroll with my loving pet would suddenly turn into a titanic struggle for survival. Mine. Wolf was an animal of great strength and enormous front feet with wide spreading toes which gave him the leverage of Saint George's dragon. The gripping power of these feet he used—always unexpectedly—to change directions very suddenly, and he would tear off in every and all ways at once. This was the impression I got as I was pulled flat and taut.

One golden morning this abrupt tactic broke my wristwatch, my glasses, and three of my best ribs.

The fact that I used two choke collars and a heavily linked truck tow chain (the weight of which alone would bring a yoke of oxen to its knees) disturbed him not a bit. He seemed to be inspired by it. It was a challenge to his strength and stamina. He knew that someday he would stretch those fantastically tensiled steel links until they would fly apart like a string of

J. C. Penney beads. And *he* knew that *I* knew he could do it.

Then there were some mornings when it was a pleasure to take this super brute for his constitutional. He'd act as cooperative as any fawning cocker spaniel, and just as affectionate. During these blessed times he wouldn't pull me along like he was dragging a sea anchor in a hurricane. He would walk quietly by my side, and every once in a while he would reach out to take my hand gently between his murderous-looking fangs to reassure me that everything was going to be all right—the wolves of the world had everything under control.

But these quiescent mornings were infrequent. Most of the time our woodland rambles were tests of durability for me and practice attacks for him. His attack rehearsals, I assumed, were just in case we ran into a decrepit old moose in the hills of Connecticut and Wolf would have to do his part in bringing him down. Which was all very well for *him*, but I didn't like *my* part as the decrepit old moose. Wolf, using the same tactical approach as he would with an aged moose, circled me endlessly, slashing at my pants' legs, and occasionally going in a bit deeper than the faded corduroy. The occasional gouges I didn't mind, but the circling with Wolf, the wolf, on one end of the chain leash and me on the other, spinning at 78 rpm, did something to my equilibrium. It destroyed it. My whole world started spinning crazily and my only defense was to try to grab his mouth and hang on. This seemed to discourage him—it didn't seem to hurt him—however tight I ground his teeth against his lips.

I don't think there is any way to hurt a full-grown wolf in hand-to hand combat, but the mouth grip gave him a chance to think it over, and he usually decided to go back to sniffing and investigating everything in sight or rolling in every foul-smelling mess he found along the way (he could give fifteen minutes to a dead frog alone).

The walking of a wolf was a task. A burden. A chore—to say the least. *Why* did I do it? Did I do it for *love?*

17

Am I an animal *nut?* Did I do it for *him* or *me?* I don't *know* why I did it. Or why I *had* to *have* a *wolf!*

Years ago I was barnstorming across Texas with a small musical group. I was the drummer and also the driver and owner of a 1932 Ford runabout in which I carried my drums and the musical group. Driving across Texas is an adventure unto itself, let alone in a 1932 Ford runabout with solid tires and a radiator which had never known the sweet taste of water for more than three hours at a time. This radiator didn't just leak, as we careened through the tiny hamlets of southwest Texas, it *flushed sidewalks.* You could *shower* by it. *This* idea held, of course, no attraction for a small musical group touring southwest Texas. *Bathing* never entered our minds! But keeping the radiator comparatively or even slightly slaked never left the consciousness of even the most carefree of our small musical group, which, incidentally, was known as Bonnie and the Three Clydes —which is exactly what we looked like. We had been arrested at least forty-seven times on suspicion alone. Suspicion of *what* they never told us, but when we all looked into a cracked motel room mirror as a group— we knew they had good reason.

We looked capable of *anything!* And we were—except music. But to the good folk of southwest Texas we were Lawrence Welk, Clyde McCoy, and Enoch Light. There was no television in those days and *we* were in color (which is more than you can say about southwest Texas).

One day, along about sundown, as they say in southwest Texas, we reached the small town of Riverbend, which, in my opinion, was the most misnomered town in all of southwest Texas. There was no bend because there was no river. This worried us no little because the radiator of my 1932 Ford runabout was white hot and as waterless as Riverbend turned out to be. It was a ghost town, and as romantic as it looked in the purpling twilight—it also looked ominous. We of Bonnie and the Three Clydes could picture our four grinning skulls staring with eyeless sockets at a rusting and unhinged Texaco station sign while the haunted desert wind sang, "You can trust your car to the man who wears the star."

There was nothing to do but to go on and pray to Saint Jude for a not-too-far filling station or a stray cowboy with loaded kidneys. Saint Jude must have been listening, even if the man with the star wasn't, as we chugged around a bend (which also didn't contain a river) and ran smack into Joe's gas station and lion farm.

Joe was very glad to see us. I think he would have been equally glad to see an Indian war party—or the contagious Father Damien—or Godzilla.

"Howdy, folks," Joe said. "For fifty cents I'll get in the cage with the lions." Then he stood, a shy smile trying to break through his wind-weathered face. "Might even do it for a quarter," Joe continued. "Nothing to worry about. Lions as tame as kittens." This last was accompanied by a gesture with bloody-bandaged right hand to more or less picture a tame kitten.

"What happened to your hand?" Bonnie, whose real name was Selma, said.

"Oh," Joe explained, hiding his bandaged hand behind him, "just a scratch—I'm a bleeder. Least little thing—I bleed. Look at me cross-eyed—I bleed."

Bennie Koch, our banjo player, who was cross-eyed, said, "Lemme through."

"Now wait a minute, Bennie," I said. "We just stopped for water and maybe a coupla gallons of gas—"

"You mean," Joe the filling man said, the tears welling up in his tired green-gray eyes, "you ain't gonna let me go into the lions' cage? How about fifteen cents?—a dime?"

"Look," I said, "I don't even know what you're talking about. What cage? What lions? Where?"

"Right out in the back of the station," Joe said. "I got 'em in cages out there—fifteen lions."

"Mountain lions? From around here?" I asked.

"No, no," Joe said. "These are African lions—from Africa. Full grown. Big lions—that's why I hafta charge to go in with them."

19

"You're kidding," Bonnie, whose real name was Selma, said.

"Not that I wouldn't go in there for nothing," Joe continued. "I gotta—sometime—to feed 'em and tidy up a bit."

"Fifteen lions," Bennie said. "Must be quite a bit of 'tidying up a bit,' huh?" Then he laughed like the moronic banjo player that he was.

"Come on, I'll show ya," Joe said and started off into the dimming recesses in the rear of his filling station. When I saw it, I couldn't believe it. In back of the crumbling station in what must have been the place where old cars go to die (there were hundreds of bashed wrecks) was the lion cage! With fifteen full-grown African lions! Sleek, fat, and sassy. The cage, which didn't look strong enough to contain a determined guinea hen, seemed to contain the lions very well. The whole area must have taken in at least an acre and was provided with weather shelters and a few well-clawed and shredded stumps which must have once been fairly good-sized trees. There was wire netting over the whole area, which any intelligent lion knew would not impede him in the least if he decided to leap through it, but apparently these lions had no thought of insurrection or escape. When they saw Joe they all clustered around a sagging wood and wire gate, shouldering each other aside to get closer to the apparently beloved caressing touch of Joe, who had forgotten about his potential patrons and was giving his all to scratching as many leonine ears as he could with two leathery hands stretched through the overstressed cage wire.

I thought the wire was in immediate danger of parting, and Bonnie and the Three Clydes had a fifty-dollar job at the Dreamland Ballroom in Fart's Crossing which was still twenty miles away, so I said, "Joe, we need some gas and water. We gotta go."

"Huh?" Joe said, dragging himself back to the real world. "What about the lions? Come on—only fifty cents —maybe they'll attack me!" This last he said with what passed for glee.

"I'm sorry," I said, "but as much as we'd all like to

20

see you attacked by the lions, we just haven't got any extra fifty centses to go throwing around with such wild abandon."

"Okay," Joe said, touching a dirty rag to his nose and turning his head away from us. "Come on—the gas is out front, and there's water in a watering can. There's a Coke machine, too, but the dust was too much—it'll take your nickel but it won't give you nothin' for it."

During the half-filling of the gas tank and the futile pourings of liquid into the radiator, I got the story of the lions from Joe. He didn't have the lions because he could charge fifty cents to go into the cage with them. He had the lions because he loved them, and he was rapidly going broke trying to make enough money from his pitiful little gas station and tow car business to feed them. It had all started, he told me, when someone told him about a circus that had gone bankrupt in some nearby town, and they were going to shoot the lions because no one was going to feed them and they didn't know what else to do with them. People in southwest Texas had enough trouble feeding themselves.

There were only seven lions to begin with, but Joe didn't know how, or didn't want to know how, to separate the males from the females; so he didn't try. And lions have no qualms about breeding in captivity and have a go at each other any old time they feel like it, which is fun for the lions but rough on the budget. *Anybody's* budget. Soon the lions were eating better than Joe, was, or at least more regularly. He had tried to get the University of Texas interested in what he called the Southwest Texas Lion Experimental Station. "But they wouldn't go for it nohow," Joe said. "They knew I just wanted 'em as just pets."

"Could you put 'em in a zoo and go and visit with them once in a while?" I suggested, knowing all along that this was a lousy suggestion. Zoos weren't that anxious to receive fifteen lions—all in one gift-wrapped package. Most zoos didn't have enough room, and most zoos, even in the largest of cities, didn't have the kind of zoo budget it would have taken to feed fifteen lions—not every day, anyway. And on the days they didn't feed them the indignant roarings would be heard for miles around. I remember this from my early days in Los Angeles when the great entertainment before Disneyland and topless-bottomless waitresses was a place called Gay's Lion Farm located in El Monte, a sleepy little town a short trolley ride from downtown L.A. At Gay's they didn't feed the lions on Mondays—to keep them "in good shape," they explained.

This withholding of the horsemeat hors d'oeuvres *did* keep the lions in excellent shape, but it just *ruined* El Monte's Mondays. The lions, and there must have been a hundred of them, roared all through the day and all through the night until dawn on Tuesdays when the normal room service was restored. This was the start of the now vast California psychiatry conglomerate—from a few hundred nervous breakdowns in tiny El Monte to the entire Western seaboard, from Malibu to the mountains, and from the Mexican border to the Columbia River.

"*You* want a coupla lions," Joe said, as he tried to wipe my sandpitted windshield clean with a grease-laden hand towel.

I *did* want a couple of lions, but in those days I had more willpower than I am able to generate now, and I said no.

"Maybe we *should* take a couple of lions," Bonnie, whose real name I've forgotten, said. "Might make a nice group." Then she gestured like she was creating a marquee sign and said, "Bonnie and the Three Clydes and Two Lions."

"I *like* that," Bennie, the banjo player. said.

"You also like Eleanor Roosevelt," Slim Moyston said. Slim Moyston was our piano player. This was an assumption. We *had* to assume it because that's what he told us when we first met in a bar. Thus far on this swing through southwest Texas we'd had no proof because Slim not only smoked some kind of nonhabit-forming grass, he also drank absinthe. The *real* thing—which has been prohibited in every civilized country on the globe. Where Slim obtained his everflowing supply we never learned, but we knew it was everflowing because Slim's tongue had long ago turned green. These charming habits of Slim's were a very real deterrent to his ever playing the piano for us when we wanted him to.

"I *love* Eleanor Roosevelt," Bennie said. "You just don't know how much good she's done us black folks."

"Holy Christ!" Bonnie said, shaking her oversprayed head. "Here we go with that 'black folks' routine again!"

"What's wrong with that?" Bennie said, not at all disturbed by Bonnie's annoyance.

"You're *not black,* you dumb bastard! You're just *stupid!*" Bonnie had suddenly begun to scream.

"On second thought," Joe said, "maybe I'd better keep them two lions—I don't want them in no broken home."

"They're not married," I said, indicating Bonnie and Bennie, who by this time were getting ready to spit at each other.

"That's even *worse,*" Joe said. "That'll be two dollars and seventy-six cents. I gotta charge you for all that water because I gotta haul it in here in a water wagon. Almost ten miles."

"That's all right," I said. "I sure wish I could take a couple of lions off your hands."

"Aw," Joe said, "it would never work—I'd be sorry. I know I would. I'd want 'em back. I guess—I guess I just love 'em. And *that's* not gonna end." Then he turned away from me and went back into the shambles of his tiny office and lit a kerosene lamp. He looked much older than he was and tired, too.

Many years have passed since that lonely night in the vast, dry reaches of southwest Texas. I've often wondered what happened to Joe and his lions, but I really don't want to know.

Maybe *this* is why I had a wolf. Maybe I've got what Joe had. That strange bond between animals and man.

23

3

AT a party or any sort of gathering, someone always points me out as the freak who has a wolf,
and invariably someone tries to top me in my taste in
fauna by announcing, *seriously,* that they have a schnauzer. It's very difficult for me not to say, "Oh really? Is
it tame?" Or, "I didn't know you could domesticate a
schnauzer!" Or, "You better be careful—I understand that
when they get a little older they *turn.*"

I suppose I really am a target, for having such exotic animals as a mountain lion and a wolf, but I never
gave this aspect of it a second thought before now. Why
is a wolf or a mountain lion so unusual as a pet? Do
people think that dogs and cows and chickens and goats
and ducks and horses have always been domesticated?
That they just came out of the forests and the jungles
and started to follow people home one fine night?

True, a wolf or a mountain lion is not seen much in
downtown Milwaukee, but all over the United States
many, many families have wolves, mountain lions, coyotes,
bears, raccoons, ocelots, jaguars, and many other kinds
of "different" creatures as pets. Some of these families
can't cope too well with the exigencies of owning such
pets and have had to give them up. These are usually
people who have not read up enough on the animal
they want to adopt and run into trouble because the animal doesn't act "average"—average being acting like a
dog or a cat or a horse or a cow.

Once I tried to challenge a schnauzer owner who was
not aware he was talking to a Wolf Man. This happened
in Honansville, Connecticut, our now hometown.

"I understand you have a schnauzer?" I said to this
hearty martini drinker one trivial night at the Honansville
Cultural Center. The Honansville Cultural Center had
been started some ten or so years ago by the good

citizens of Honansville who felt the need for culture in order to live the full life. But culture had soon dropped by the way after a few string quartets and a half dozen lectures concerned with Stanley's expedition to find Livingstone, Robert Peary's discovery of the North Pole assisted by four Eskimos and Matt Henson, a *negro,* which gave most of the liberals a warm glow, and the final lecture which dealt with sex in the Victorian era—a subject which didn't give *anybody* a warm glow. From then on the members of the Honansville Cultural Center got their warm glow in the only way most of them knew. Booze. And lots of it. Which was quite all right on those long icy winter nights—it gave them something to do on the ride home—mainly trying to figure out who was driving. Sometimes nobody was, and this led to some nasty clean-up jobs for the cops when the little old station wagon didn't quite make the curve on the Lovers' Leap road. (I often wonder what a station wagon full of happy, laughing drunks think about when they suddenly find themselves halfway down the 700-foot drop to the bottom of Lovers' Leap gorge. They probably think it's just an air pocket and go right on being happy and laughing and drunk. Which is really as good a way to go as any.)

"Oh, yes, I *do* have a schnauzer," Mr. Rogers Dotson said. "Are you familiar with the breed?" I didn't dare say no, because I knew before dawn I would hear much much more than I cared to know about the schnauzer, so I said, "Yes."

Mr. Dotson, who was pure tweed, was quite unhappy about this; but after downing a full double martini, including a pickled onion (toothpick and all), and not interrupting the beginning of his screed any more than a comma would, he took off like a mile relay team running all four quarters himself.

He began with the origination of the schnauzer back in ancient Egypt where it had started out, he lowered his voice confidentially, "as a cat."

Mr. Dotson skillfully backed me into a corner from which there was no escape and held me enthralled by his fulsome knowledge of the schnauzer down through the ages. I was so enthralled I was toying seriously with the idea of secretly breaking the glass on my wristwatch and quietly opening my veins with a jagged edge. My life would slowly ooze away and Mr. Dotson's monotone would fade in the distance and soon I would belong to the ages. But before I could act on this brilliant solution, many moons passed and somewhere out in some faraway limbo area where I lay floating face down I heard Mr. Dotson drone a question. "Do you own a schnauzer, sir?"

"No," I said, startled that I should be included in his conversation. "Do you have an empty pocket?" Now it was Dotson's turn to be startled. "Yes—I believe so—why?"

"Because," I said, unzipping my fly, "if I'm gonna spend my life with you I gotta take a leak."

Mr. Dotson quickly buttoned every button on his Norfolk jacket and headed back to the bar, walking up and over *Mrs.* Dotson, who hadn't quite made it to the bar. Mrs. Dotson didn't seem to mind. She just mumbled something about "culture" and fell asleep with her head on her own lap.

4

FOR almost three years, my darling little Japanese wife, Reiko, and our two sons, Bobby nine and Timothy two, had lived in the rugged wilderness of northern Canada. Timothy had been born there on a blizzardy Christmas Eve in a makeshift tent halfway to the hospital—116 miles away. And Tanuki, my first and much loved wolf, had died there. Now we were living in the more-or-less rural part of northwestern Connecticut. We still had Bobby and Timothy, Chibi, an Alaskan malamute, Doggie, a 4-pound Pomeranian, and Pussycat, a 200-pound mountain lion, but we didn't have a wolf, which to me was very disturbing. Almost everyone goes around saying. "What is home without a mother?" which can be answered very simply—you save a helluva lot of money on Whitman Samplers. "What is home without a wolf?" was *my* problem.

The howl of a wolf in the middle of a cold, clear winter's night is to me like all the beautiful sounds in the world blended into one. It's a truly melancholy sound, like the far-off whistle of a lonely freight puffing its way across the great. empty. windswept icy plains of North Dakota. Melancholy and sad, but sweet, musical and poignant, filled with the echoes of a long-ago age. A wolf howl sounds like something which must have been heard since the dawn of man. Which, I guess, it has. But, alas, may not be heard at man's inevitable supersonic fade-out from this precious planet.

The howl of a wolf may not thrill some people. It may scare them silly. as it did our immediate ancestors who landed at Plymouth Rock in 1620. In a very limited time there wasn't a wolf left in all of New England, and Indians were in short supply also. The Pilgrims, or Puritans (you have a choice in what you want to call them), in order to escape persecution in England had come here to try a little of it themselves. A wolf howl in 1620 could only mean one thing to these people—trouble! They had heard the story of Little Red Riding Hood repeated so many times they believed it. Later on, when they had more leisure, they started to believe in *witches*—which led to some great fun for the Pilgrims and the Puritans.

These early New England folk had heard nothing evil about the Indians—Little Red Riding Hood hadn't met Sitting Bull or Crazy Horse on her way to Grandma's house—but somehow the Indians just didn't *fit* into the early settlers' Currier & Ives picture of little old New England. Besides, *they* had the best land and didn't know what to do with it except hunt and fish and plant corn in it. The early New Englanders soon fixed that. They made "treaties" with the Indians, which was like giving an Australian aborigine a GMAC new Chevy contract and asking him to sign it and put down his Social Security number.

27

The Indians signed everything, accepted the generous gifts of beads, dime-store hatchets, and tuberculosis, and soon found themselves in Ohio—wondering what the hell happened after that first Thanksgiving.

But this isn't a history book. History books are written by men who have never known Raquel Welch. I have never known Raquel Welch either, which she will live to regret. I have known Reiko Hashimoto for almost twelve years now, and if nothing else she is consistent. She's beautiful, too, and kind and considerate and loving, and everything else that a man could want—except she doesn't like animals. Or maybe I should say she doesn't like the idea of *me* having animals—not just wild or exotic animals, but dogs and cats as well. In this she is consistent. *Very* consistent!

"No wolf!" Reiko said, slightly louder than Otto Preminger would have said it to his lowest underling. Reiko was not the tender little Lotus Blossom I had believed I'd be getting when we were married eleven or so years ago. She *was* Otto Preminger, with a dash of Genghis Khan and a Marine drill instructor with a boil. She didn't pitter patter around in soft little brocaded slippers—she stomped around in hobnailed boots, waving a cattle prod and giving orders like she was in command of the Pacific Fleet.

"Wow!" Harry Mitchell, our down-the-road neighbor, said. "I didn't know you could be so positive, Reiko."

"Women are always positive when it comes to animals, Harry," I said. "Women just don't like animals." I knew whereof I spoke on this subject, having had some experience with other wives.

"That's not true," Ruthie Mitchell, Harry's semilovely wife, said. "We have a cat and a dog and I *adore* them."

"How come you won't let 'em in the house?" Harry asked as a plainly noncombatant, then disappeared instantly into the kitchen to sweeten up his drink.

"I *do* let them into the house," Ruthie said to Reiko and me. but mostly to me. "Of course," she continued, "I spray the whole house with Dog-off and Cat-off just before I do—you know, in case of—well—accidents."

28

"That's an idea," I said. "Maybe they also have Wolf-off."

"No wolf!" Reiko repeated, as Harry came back from the kitchen and threw himself into *my* easy chair with what I thought was an unnecessarily overcompensated proprietary air.

"Wolves are smarter than dogs," I said, which was not a good point, but I had to try to defend my position no matter how much it exposed the weaknesses of my case and my language.

"Who cares?!" Reiko said.

"I agree with Reiko," Ruthie Mitchell said. "Who cares *what* a wolf is! Why can't you settle for a dog? Or a cat? Or a—"

"Or an electric eel," Harry Mitchell said. "I understand they make wonderful pets."

"Harry," I said, "go sweeten your drink."

"And not only that—you don't hafta take 'em for walks."

"Or spray the whole house with Eel-off," I said.

"What the hell is Eel-off?" Harry said, trying in vain to bring forth a malignant belch. Before I could answer, if there *was* an answer, Reiko repeated, "No wolf!"

We were sitting in the living room of our new home in Honansville, the teeny-tiny village in the northwest corner of Connecticut. The evening had been fairly pleasant. Reiko was always the perfect hostess, which was something she hadn't lost from her early family training in Japan. Whenever we had friends for dinner, Reiko never stopped smiling. She treated our guests as if nothing could give her greater pleasure than being of service and seeing to their every desire. I don't know whether she actually felt this, because when we were alone she always said she didn't want any neighbors (which I assumed also meant people dropping in for dinner—people like Harry and Ruthie Mitchell), but when we had guests (invited or not) she was the Galloping Gourmet and Florence Nightingale and Madame Butterfly.

Reiko wanted no neighbors in Honansville because they were available. When we live, as we still do on

29

occasion, deep in the Canadian wilderness, she bitches because it's too lonely and we have no neighbors. What's a mother to do?????

Things were sort of quieting down this particular evening. Harry was getting pleasantly mulled on the Seven Star scotch, which my liquor distributor brother from Buffalo had thoughtfully provided. Ruthie, who looked a little like Mae Murray with her bee-stung lips (a lip style that went out with rolled stockings and chastity for the poor), amused herself with double brandies and snatches of old barrack ballads she'd learned from her father, whom she said had been with Ronald Colman at the Khyber Pass.

Reiko, in order to liven up the party (if that's what it was), again repeated, "No wolf!"

"Jesus Christ!" I said. "What's *with* you? Look—I don't drink or smoke or run around all night looking for chicks —so what the hell is wrong with wanting to have a little wolf for a pet?"

"Maybe it would be better if you drank and smoked and ran around with chicks," Harry suggested, dropping three inches of cigar ash on our non-highly polished plywood floor. Reiko with superb bad timing nudged an ashtray toward him.

"No, thank you, Reiko," Harry said. "I couldn't eat another thing."

"That's an ashtray," Ruthie said. "Reiko wants you to use it."

"Oh," Harry said. "What a *droll* idea. Reiko, you're *droll*, do you know that?"

"What's that?" Reiko said.

"What's what?" Harry said.

"Droll? What's *droll?*"

"*I* am," Harry said. "*I'm* droll and *you're* Japanese." This triggered a giggling paroxysm in Harry. He giggled and hurled and snorted and fought a losing skirmish for control of his amusement and admiration of his superb sense of the comedic.

"Jesus Christ!" I said to Ruthie. "That Harry Mitchell of yours is *really dull!*"

"Yeah," Ruthie agreed, "but he's great in the hay. In

bed he's dull, but in the hay—nice, clean alfalfa and it's like an aphrodisiac with Harry. Harry, were you brought up on a farm?"

"Yeah," Harry said, with an unforgivable chortle. "And I was born in a manger."

"See, I toldja," Ruthie said.

"What?" I said.

"Yeah," Harry said, sensing an attentive ear, "I was born in a manger—because of my father."

"What the hell are you talking about?" I said, sorry that I had given up drinking so early in life.

"His *father!*" Ruthie said.

"I *heard* him!" I said.

"Yeah," Harry said, "my father was a little far out—he was an *Eighth* Day Adventist. He made the whole family dramatize Bible stories."

"And *that's* how you came to be born in a manger?" I said.

"Yeah," Harry said, getting up and heading for the bottle in the kitchen, "that's the way it happened."

"I toldja," Ruthie said. "A little new-mown alfalfa and Harry's Errol Flynn back from the great beyond."

"No wolf!" Reiko said, feeling this was her only chance to get back into our living-room talk show.

And that's the way it was left until the wolf arrived. Three weeks later.

5

I HAD told Reiko, as I took off from our mountaintop home one bright June morning, that I was going to New York to meet with Dick Crenna, who was planning a movie based on *Shut Up and Eat Your Snowshoes!*—a book I had written a year or so before about our experiences living in the Canadian north country. She was happy about this because she could not understand why none of my previous books had ever

31

been made into a movie. *I* couldn't understand this either. I had written seven books, including my autobiography, which was mostly about my twenty years in Hollywood and contained a lot of good movie material. My life was just *chock full* of good standard movie plots, including a lot of good standard violence, good standard intrigue, good standard suspense, good standard love, good standard sex, and good standard movie starlets who always wore black patent leather tap shoes with big white bows, and who always left me (in real life) for a chance at stardom. Little did they know that if they had waited *long enough* I could have put in a good word for them with Mr. David Merrick, whom I met just last week sitting alone at a table for one at the Roseland Ballroom in New York. Mr. Merrick isn't casting at the moment, so maybe meeting *him* wouldn't thrill the movie starlets I knew when I was a Hollywood extra, and also Mr. Merrick might not get icy fingers running up and down *his* spine meeting some fifty-year-old movie starlet still wearing black patent leather tap shoes and big white bows either.

Anyway, Mr. Crenna is going to make *Shut Up and Eat Your Snowshoes!* into a movie, and Mr. Crenna is going to play me. *He's* going to play *me* instead of me playing *me* because *he* looks more like *me* than *I* look like *me*. Actually, I am very happy that he is going to play me. And, I might add, to get one of my books made into a movie, I would be happy if *Flip Wilson* played me. Or better still, if he played *Reiko*.

This positive action, this very movement of getting up and going to New York pleased Reiko very much. She never could quite fathom what I was doing all day in my little office if she didn't hear the typewriter gunning out thousands of money-begetting words. She didn't seem to understand, as hundreds of writers' wives down through the years haven't understood, that when a writer is staring out the window, walking lonely walks in the woods, or painting a watercolor of the Santa Barbara Mission—he's working. Maybe.

I had told Reiko the truth about going to New York, but I hadn't told her about the detour. The detour to

Old Lady Simpson's. Old Lady Simpson raised wolves and lived near an abandoned iron mine at the end of a long, dead-end, dirt road about fifty miles from Honansville. Old Lady Simpson was to be my last chance to get a wolf puppy this year. I had exhausted every other possible source.

The day was warm and sunny. The back roads I had to drive to find Old Lady Simpson were narrow and winding and very New England picturesque. The back country still contained farms and farmers who had not yet been approached by any advance scouts for development blight, a condition by which Connecticut is rapidly being devoured. Most of the farms around Honansville had succumbed, and the lovely old weatherbeaten, semiwhite farmhouses were being torn down to make room for six split-levels, or they were being "lovingly restored" to be lovingly sold for twice their worth to some unsuspecting city dweller who wants to get back to the land—even if it's only an acre.

As I thought I was getting closer to Old Lady Simpson's, although I was not quite sure, I almost ran into five thousand cows. I rounded a bend in the dusty path which wasn't marked thus on the map and there they were, crossing the road from one pasture to another. Leisurely. Very leisurely, and the farmer, who was at parade rest under a huge elm, probably the last elm left on earth, was chewing a long straw and looking off into the hazed distance. There was a man, I thought, who was actually *relaxed*. Something you don't see too much of anymore.

I shut off the engine and waited for the bovine Big Parade to pass. After a few minutes, the endless, formless line of cows continued to block my way, so I got out and walked over to the farmer, who seemed not in the least concerned with the terrible onrush of time. Or anything else.

The farmer acknowledged my presence with an almost imperceptible nod and continued to chew his straw.

"Nice bunch of cows," I said (what else are you going to say about a nice bunch of cows?).

"Yeah," the farmer agreed, "nice bunch of cows."

There was a sort of too long pause, I felt, so I said, "Get much milk from 'em?"

"Yeah," the farmer said, "if they're fresh."

"Uh-huh," I said, "fresh milk, eh?" The farmer took a long look at me and then at my station wagon, which was fairly new and had just been washed. Then he said, not unkindly, "You don't know much about cows, do you?"

"No," I said, "I'm a writer. Do you know Old Lady Simpson?"

"Holy Christ!" the farmer said.

"I understand she's got wolves," I said. "She raises 'em."

"Yeah. She's got wolves all right—about five miles up the road. On still nights I can hear 'em howling."

"Gee," I said, "must be a thrill. Wolves right here in Connecticut."

"Yeah," the farmer said.

"How many?" I said. "How many wolves has she got?"

"Oh—fifty or sixty."

"Wow!"

"Yeah."

"Do the neighbors ever complain?" I asked. I wanted to know more about how people felt toward wolves.

"What neighbors?" the farmer said.

6

AS I drove down Old Lady Simpson's private road, which had to be the worst road in all of North America, I tried to imagine what Old Lady Simpson, who raised wolves, would look like. In my mind's eye I pictured her, as I continued to gouge the rear end of my car on huge boulders which seemed to raise up their jagged heads just as my differential was about to pass over them (I certainly didn't see them beforehand), as about sixty years old, complete with mustache

34

and snaggled teeth—with maybe a large wart on the side of her eagled nose. A large wart with a thicket of gray hair growing from it like a stunted cactus. Her eyes would be rheumy and of no particular color. Spittle would drip out of one side of her bloodless lips, which she would wipe away with the back of her liver-blotched hand. She would be dressed in dirty, torn Levis and a filthy man's shirt, held around her by safety pins. She would be a mess! But if she had a wolf puppy for me, she would be beautiful.

As I got near Old Lady Simpson's house, the road dropped sharply to a rather swift little stream, which apparently could be forded. I gunned hell out of the station wagon and, sure enough, I got stuck right in the middle of the stream, inadvertently leaning on the horn with my elbow. Immediately fifty or sixty wolves very close by, it seemed, raised their heads and let go. It was the Mormon Tabernacle Choir of wolfdom. Long and low and lonely. My whole body was suddenly chillingly thrilled to the point of instant ecstasy! What a lovely sound! A lovely, lovely sound!

Old Lady Simpson's house was something else. And the ascent of her front porch steps would make Edmund Hillary think twice, or back down entirely. I'm quite sure when I put pressure on the first step the house tilted. The house itself made Charles Addams' creations take on the look of a new development at Key Biscayne. There wasn't a window that wasn't boarded or papered or tinned up. The ridge pole had long ago given up and fallen in, and the runoff of rain water had ravished the entire roof into a series of green mold-choked miniature canyons capable, in the rainy season, of serving as fish weirs. Or small beaver ponds for small beavers. Or rice paddies for organic food nuts. The house, as a unit, was the most devastated, ruinous pile of decaying desolation I have ever seen. I was glad to be there *that* day because I knew it wouldn't last another.

Old Lady Simpson was not quite what I had expected. She was a wildly stunning beauty. Green *green* eyes. Thick copper-red hair roiling down her back to the bottom of her hot pants, which were nowhere near the bottom of her bottom. Long dancer's legs, and hard, high breasts straining against the thin, almost see-through cashmere sweater. They moved when she moved. My jaw felt as if it had dropped down to my sneakers. I was Mickey Rooney in a Judge Hardy movie. I was a tongue-tied, dry-mouthed adolescent on my first date (with the opposite sex). After what must have seemed like hours to her (days to me), I managed to croak, "Is your—*mother*—home?"

"My mother lives in Beverly Hills," she said, in the most libidinal voice I have ever heard. She sounded like an orgasm set to music.

"Oh," I said, loosening up a little, but not too much. "Are you—?"

"I'm Old Lady Simpson," the Goddess said.

"But—"

"I'm thirty-one."

"But—" I repeated, brilliantly.

"This place," the Goddess said, "is called Old Lady Simpson's after my grandmother. She lived to be ninety-eight. She was born in this house."

"Oh," I said, getting my breath back slowly. "Mighty nice place."

"Yes," she said, "like something Al Capp would draw —if he was depicting a depression in Lower Slobbovia."

"Well—it could do with a little—er, paint."

"That's all that's holding it together now," she said with a touch of sadness, then, quickly changing gears, "May I help you?"

I counted the ways she could help me, but I said, "Are you the 'wolf' lady?"

She smiled a beautiful smile. "Yes—I'm the wolf lady. But I don't look like the wolf lady, do I? And you'd like to know what I'm doing way back here in the woods, all by myself, raising wolves—wouldn't you?"

I had to admit it. "Yes," I said. "I didn't expect a Playmate of the Month—I expected a crone."

"Everybody does," the Goddess said.

I somehow wished she had been a crone. She was delicious to look at, but it was easier to talk to a crone. Crones don't jiggle.

"I raise wolves because I love wolves and I want to see them preserved just as long as possible. Do you want a wolf?"

"I sure do," I said. I must have said this with a little more emotion than I had intended, because the Goddess laughed. And jiggled. And my heart went pitty-pat —like Big Ben at noon. All my life I've been a pushover for jiggling goddesses. Then I thought about Reiko. She didn't jiggle. Japanese parents were very strict about this.

"Come on in," Miss Simpson said, opening the front door carefully. Very carefully. The door had only one hinge, which hadn't been oiled since the Revolution. When things had quieted down again, Miss Simpson said, "This way—he's out in the kitchen."

Then she led me through a dank hallway to a room that had to be the kitchen. It contained an iron woodstove and a refrigerator which must have been put together by Edison and Henry Ford one day when they didn't know what the hell they were inventing. There was a table with a leg missing and two drunken wooden chairs. The floor, where it wasn't patched with flattened pieces of an oil drum, was 1912 linoleum patched with 1908 linoleum and festooned with throw rugs made from the New York *Times* Sunday edition.

"This is the kitchen," she said.

"You're kidding." She looked at me a long time before she said or did anything else, then she reached down behind the woodstove and picked up a nondescript little animal. It was sort of a gray-black with bluish eyes, a ratty tail, and a short, pushed-in nose.

"What the hell's that?" I said.

"A beautiful little wolf puppy."

"Oh, come on!"

"This is the way they *all* look at three weeks."

"Where's his nose? I thought wolves have long, pointy noses."

"What did your nose look like when you were three weeks old?" she said.

"It was long and pointy." I couldn't lie. Miss Simpson returned the little animal to its little box behind the stove and said, "Come on—I want to introduce you to that little puppy's mother and father. Follow me. You're going to get a big surprise." Then, catching the sudden twitch of my head, "—wolf-wise."

"Okay," I said, and once again followed her magnificent, and provocative, rear down another long, dark, and dank corridor. She opened a door and there it all was. The wolf pit, or, I guess you'd say, wolf kennel. To me at first glance it seemed like we were surrounded by hundreds of silent, glowering wolves, but there weren't that many and they weren't glowering. They were just on the alert.

"They look as if they're on guard," I said.

"They are."

"They're beautiful." And they were, all colors, gray, black, brown, white, and some almost red. We stopped next to a pen where two of the most magnificent specimens of wolfdom were enclosed. The female, Miss Simpson explained, was the black one, and the larger wolf a huge male and came from Alaska—that is, his antecedents did. The Alaskan species, she explained, was the *second* largest of all the world's wolves, but *this* one, so far as *I* was concerned, was the largest. He must have weighed in at least 150 pounds. What a gorgeous brute!.

"Now," Miss Simpson said, "Do *they* look like *wolves?*"

"They are the wolfiest wolves I have ever seen," I said.

"Well, that's what your pup will look like in a year or so."

"*My* pup? You mean that little gray thing there in back of the stove is gonna look like his papa there?" I said.

"I think he's going to look even better than his papa," Miss Simpson said. "Better—and bigger!" I almost swooned.

On the drive home, with the little wolf in a cardboard carton on the seat next to me, I forgot about Dick Crenna's movie completely. I even forgot about the strange Miss Simpson's lovely everythings. That's what wolves can do to you.

38

7

"I THINK I go back Japan!" That was Reiko's welcome to the little wolf puppy. This is Reiko's standard reaction when anything departs from the norm. And bringing a wolf into the house was not her idea of the *Cho-cho-san* thing to do.

"What's this big expostulatory attitude?" I said. Then I had to spend fifteen minutes explaining "expostulatory attitude." After she understood about as well as she ever would, I decided to become wily, tricky, and devious, and clever. I said, "It's a present, dear—a present for you—for Mother's Day." I guess I wasn't wily, tricky, and devious enough because that night for dessert Reiko put soy sauce on my apple pie à la mode.

"What the hell is this?" I said.

"For Father's Day," she explained, looking at me with nothing but innocence in her lovely brown eyes.

"Are you trying to be inscrutable?" I said.

"What's inscrutable?" Bobby, my number-one son, asked. Bobby, my number-one son, seized on any and all opportunities to attach himself to any and all adult conversations.

"Your mother—she's inscrutable," I explained. Bobby thought this over carefully, then said, "Oh. Papa, how do you like my drawing?" He held a piece of paper with much crayon work on it too close for me to judge what the hell it was. (Why do kids *always* do this? Do they figure your sight is so far gone your eyeballs have to *feel* instead of *see?* Or is a child's distance calculation a little on the incunabular side?)

"It's marvelous," I said, "simply *marvelous!*"

"What is it?" Bobby insisted, I thought rather loudly.

"It's *just great!*" I said.

"Great *what?*" he said, and I felt he was just short

of giving me 'a shove—like a guy in a saloon who's looking for trouble about *anything*—with *anybody*.

"Okay," I said, not wishing to get karate chopped by a third grader, "what is it?"

"It's a dinosaur—smelling its own tail," Bobby said.

"Oh."

"Don't you like it, Papa?"

"Yeah, I like it better than 'Aristotle Contemplating the Bust of Homer.' "

"Here," Bobby said, "you can have it. Hang it in your office."

"I may hang myself in my office," I said.

"You *always* have trouble with animals," Reiko said, lifting the lid off a pot of steaming rice, then slapping it back on—at the same time keeping an eye on the little wolf puppy who was sniffing the kitchen clean. "How about that time in Westport when the lion broke its leg?"

"What lion in what Westport who broke his leg?" I asked, knowing full well what lion in what Westport.

"Your play. The Westport Playhouse. The big flop!" This hurt. This went down deeper than the quick.

"Maybe it was a flop in Westport," I snarled, like an unfriendly Frank Sinatra, Junior, "but it was a *smash* in the *Poconos!*"

"What's Poconos, Papa?" Bobby said.

"Yeah," Reiko said, "what's Poconos?" I didn't try to explain. An old wound had been opened and I was too busy mentally suturing it back together. It was true. My play had been a flop in Westport (not financially) but really not, I felt, through anything *I* had or had not done. On the opening night only a few of the lesser actors knew their lines. The stars were still fumbling, and right in the middle of the first act a violent thunderstorm blacked out the entire area for twenty minutes. As soon as the lights went back on, a man in the third row had a heart attack and had to be removed from the theater during one of my best punch lines. I felt this was extremely bad taste on the part of the victim, but nevertheless I saved his life by running to my car and hauling back a tank of oxygen which I kept there for emergencies like opening nights.

40

After this Marcus Welby MD incident, I don't think many people really got back to thinking about the play they were seeing. Most of them, I felt, were more interested in seeing who would drop dead next. The entire audience for the rest of the disastrous evening looked at each other, furtively, with *delicious* trepidation.

To top off this night of horrors, a lion, which I had used extremely cleverly in my blackout of my last act, broke his leg—just when he was supposed to stroll silently through the door and onto the center of the stage. How he broke his leg was not explained to me, but his trainer, who was a quick thinker and also, apparently, an apprentice idiot, screamed, "Shove him through the window!" This screamed stage direction was not only heard by the audience inside the Westport Playhouse but by audiences in summer theaters as far away as Portland, Maine, and Long Branch, New Jersey. Shove *what* through the window? the now enthralled patrons of the jam-packed Westport Playhouse wondered. They soon found out.

There were squeals of delight when they realized that a full-grown African lion was coming through the window—propelled by some mysterious force onto a handy bar top next to the window. The squeals of delight turned almost immediately to shrieks of terror as the lion, with an agonized roar of pain, leaped from the bar onto the stage and started to advance toward the audience. The record for evacuating the Westport Playhouse still stands. Eleven seconds flat. It will stand forever.

This incident did not help the overall impression of my play, but it *was* an evening to remember.

"What the hell did *I* have to do with the lion in Westport?" I said. "It wasn't my lion and *I* didn't break its leg. It just happened to fall downstairs."

"You *love* animals," Reiko said, making it sound like I was a tumescent Wyoming sheepherder who hadn't been to town for six months.

"I love animals, too," Bobby said.

"Everybody loves animals," I said, in an unbacked sweeping statement, "and, Reiko, you're a *Buddhist*—you've got to love animals. It's part of your religion."

41

Reiko let some more steam out of Old Faithful, her boiling rice pot, then started to slice up some carrots with what looked like a samurai sword.

"I don't want a wolf in my house," Reiko said, now slicing the slicing board. This was pure temper. The serene, placid, and obeisant little Japanese Lotus Blossom? Ho! Ho! Ho! Lieutenant Pinkerton! "Supposing I was a drunk—or smoked pot—or fooled around with other women (I was back to that). Would you like *that* better than me having a *pet?*" I asked.

"I'm not interested," Reiko said, turning away from me and heading up the stairs, trailing a vacuum cleaner. The status symbol of the slave. This is woman's ultimate weapon, the vacuum cleaner. When things aren't going the way a woman wants them to, there's only one thing to do—*vacuum!* They know that to a man there is no more irritating sound than that of a revved-up vacuum cleaner.

This ended the debate for the time being, and Bobby started to roughhouse with the little wolf, who really couldn't do his part yet. He was too young and too unsteady on his legs, but he gave it a try and managed to sink his tiny sharp teeth into Bobby more than once, and then he got a vise grip on the sleeve of Bobby's shirt and in no time it was in shreds. My heart sank. This wouldn't help the little wolf's cause with Reiko. She had a thing about shredded shirt sleeves.

"Tell her you got it caught in your bicycle chain," I advised Bobby.

"Okay," he agreed, "but how did it happen—was I riding my bike upside down?"

"Perfect," I said. "That's *exactly* how it happened."

"Papa—" Bobby said.

"What?"

"You're a nut."

42

8

REIKO never became completely reconciled to once again having a wolf in the family, but she tolerated his occasional "accidents" and his frequent "attacks" on her legs and the stuffed toys of which Bobby and Timothy seemed to have an *endless* supply. Which was good because this new wolf puppy could rip a full-grown kapok-filled tiger to a pile of striped debris in no more than five minutes.

Reiko's defense of her person was a hard smack on the little wolf's nose, which is supposed to be his sensitive part, but he didn't seem to be aware of this. He just kept ripping the bottom two-thirds of her around-the-house blue jeans into streamers. In no time, everything that Reiko wore on her bottom half made her look like she was part of Carnival time in Rio.

Reiko took more and more to using her vacuum cleaner as a means of self-preservation. She zoomed the vacuum right at the wolf pup and scared him out of his wits— at first. After a short while, and as he got more agile, he treated the whole thing as a very virile game, and he'd circle the machine as he would have in the wild trying to bring down a deer or a moose.

He soon found that the Hoover itself was not good to eat, but the cord, which was the best part, could easily be separated from the machine, borne away to a quiet corner, and chewed to a pulpy mass of copper wire and rubber insulation which could never be recycled. Any attempt to take the cord away from him before it was destroyed completely was met by a ferocity which in such a tiny animal would have been cute, except for his deadly seriousness and the slashings of his tiny teeth. Here, I thought, even at that early age, was a wolf to be reckoned with. He wasn't going to be a fawner—he was going to be a dominator. The order of things was going to be done *his* way. I didn't tell Reiko, but I knew this was true.

Choosing a name for a wolf is very difficult. I don't know why. Maybe it's because you can't use a cute name which would fit when the wolf is a puppy—and cute—because they grow up to look regal and noble, and a regal and noble wolf called Poopsie just doesn't work.

We called our first wolf Tanuki, which is a Japanese word meaning "raccoon." This may seem, on the surface, to be a curious fact, but it was done with reason. We had a malamute we called Chibi, and we wanted something that would sound, to a wolf, *different,* so the wolf would recognize his name when he was called. As it turned out, we could have called him Harry Truman. He never, in all the time we had him, responded to *any* name, and he would only come to me when I talked baby talk to him or enticed him with a chicken back, which he would snatch from my vulnerable fingers and dash to the farthest corner of his pen and swallow in one gulp. Even so, I felt that this new wolf should have a name.

Bobby and I came up with a few, as Reiko ignored the whole problem; and Timothy sang "Happy Birthday" to someone—this was never quite clear—from the moment he woke in the morning till he was tucked at night into his own little bed, which was also Reiko's, Bobby's and my own little bed (as per an old Japanese custom). The names Bobby and I chose and discarded were Beauty, Lobo, Rogue, Happy, Puck, Sprite, Laddie, Zeus, King, and Loco which the more we thought about it, all sounded like names of cabin cruisers tied up at a Miami Beach marina.

"Why don't you call him Garson Kanin?" suggested Harry Mitchell, who with his semilovely wife, Ruthie, had just stopped by for a three-hour drink.

"What a marvelous name!—for a wolf," Ruthie agreed. I looked at these two down-the-road neighbors, whom I loved dearly; but deep inside, I had to admit, like Miss Reardon, they did drink a little. And the drinking did not diminish their wild imaginations one bit. Still there were times when I had to question their opinions —as dangerous as it usually is to question the opinions of most drunks. The Mitchells didn't care. You could question their opinions from now on. They didn't care— or, more accurately, they didn't hear.

"Why 'Garson Kanin'?" I thought I'd ask.

"We love him," Harry said, mixing a king-sized California super salad bowl of martinis (they didn't *make* the cocktail shaker large enough for the Mitchells).

"Why?" Reiko said, not knowing who or what Garson Kanin might be, but she wanted to be part of the conversation.

"Because," Ruthie said, very sincerely, "whenever any celebrity dies, Garson Kanin has known them intimately. He writes books about them."

"Yeah," agreed Harry, stopping his alcoholic project momentarily. "Mr. Maugham—Spence and Katey—Noel Coward—"

"Noel Coward isn't dead," I said.

"Of course not," Ruthie agreed. "Garson hasn't finished his book about him yet."

"I don't think so," I said.

"Oh?" Ruthie Mitchell said archly. "*What* don't you think is so?"

"I don't think that would be a very good name for a wolf," I said.

"Oh, yes," Harry Mitchell said, "this is wolf-naming day, isn't it? I'd almost forgotten why you sent for me." Christ! I thought, when the day comes that I send for Harry Mitchell, it will be to be a pallbearer—for me, which was a grim and also unlikely thought, because I am going to live *forever* through yoga, vitamin C, wheat germ, and an injunction given me long ago by Cardinal Cushing.

"I like 'Loco,'" Bobby said, finally able to catch us adults in a rare silence.

"Loco," Timothy said, perfectly.

"'*Loco*' in Japanese means 'six,'" Reiko said.

"'Six'—that might be a good name for a wolf," Harry Mitchell said.

"I like 'Seven' better," Ruthie Mitchell said. "It's got more of the 'Call of the Wild' sound to it."

"How about 'Eight'?" I said, entering into this idiot discussion like I knew what it was all about.

A week or so later Harry Mitchell called—on the *phone,* which was a blessing in itself. "Got the perfect name for your wolf," Harry said. "I didn't know I was so good at names—"

"What's the perfect name for my wolf?" I asked, without much faith in Harry's self-given reputation for being good at names.

"Wolf," Harry said.

"What?"

"Wolf."

"Look, Harry," I said, "I think everybody will admit that it's a wolf, but I'm trying to find a name for it."

"Boy!" Harry said, with a sigh of frustration, "I sit up all night trying to think of a name for your goddamn wolf, and now you're giving me a hard time! 'Wolf'!— that's the name for your wolf—'Wolf.' "

"Oh," I said.

"Look," Harry said, steaming a little now, "you've got a dog named Dog and a cat named Cat—what's wrong with a wolf named Wolf?"

"It just—seems so simple," I said, "like calling a dog Rover. Who in hell would ever call a dog Rover?"

"I got a dog," Harry said, "and guess what his name is?"

"Rover," I guessed correctly.

"Right," Harry said, "and what's so simple about that? You know anybody else—in the world—with a dog named Rover?" I didn't.

9

SO "Wolf" it was. The little wolf now had a name, but he also had problems—his back legs had started to break down, and in a day or so he was unable to use them. He could not stand up, because of a stupid mistake on my part. I had fed the little puppy too much meat and not enough puppy chow and other things his small body needed. His condition was very much like rickets. When I read up in my *Merck Manual* what rickets was like, it scared hell out of me. I also felt very angry with myself that I could have been so totally ignorant of the wolf puppy diet, especially after I had raised his predecessor, Tanuki, from a tiny gray ball to a magnificent 140-pound wolf.

I was devastated. I was further crushed when Dr. Dann, of the Ridgefield Veterinary Hospital, chewed me out for being so dumb.

"Christ, Jack!" the doctor said. "When are you going to learn?" I was beginning to wonder myself.

I changed the little wolf's diet immediately and also started a series of enforced walkings. I would make him walk on his front legs while I held his back legs up by his tail. This was a heartbreaking sight. This tiny thing could not use his back legs at all. They just dragged. I tried long massages and a heat lamp. The massages were easy to give, but he didn't like the heat lamp at all. As helpless as he was, he would try to snap at it, but being small and helpless, he was easy to control. This treatment went on for many weeks, and as he was growing rapidly, eating the right foods, plus cod liver oil and vitamins and calcium, he became stronger and proved it by ripping long sheets of one-quarter-inch wallboard off the room where I kept him in a little guest cottage on the edge of our land. This guest cottage was some distance from the main house, and several times every day I would walk down the hill to feed the wolf and do all the other things which he needed to make him whole again.

One morning in midsummer, I entered the cottage and opened the door to the "wolf room," but Wolf wasn't there. Immediately I thought he'd been stolen. There was no other way to think. As I rushed back up the hill to telephone I don't know whom, I passed the fenced pen where we kept the malamute, and there was the little wolf—sitting on the outside of the fence, with adoring eyes fixed on Chibi.

It was a tremendous relief to know he was safe and also that he could maneuver his body the fifty yards or so between his room and the dog pen. I couldn't figure how he had escaped, unless someone had let him out. But it hadn't happened that way, I was quite sure—and knowing how clever wolves are with door latches, etc., I wanted to find out just how he had done it. So I put him back in his room and went outside where I could watch him through a small window without his seeing me. He hated his room, and I knew he would attempt an escape as soon as possible. I didn't have long to wait. As I watched, he stretched up as far as he could—which was far enough to reach the bottom sill of the window with his teeth—then pulled his body up, using his already powerful jaws and his front feet, until he could squeeze his body through the partially opened window. (I had opened it a very few inches so he would get air at night, never dreaming that he would or could make a break for liberty in his far from perfect condition.) In a few moments he was free and started to drag himself toward the dog's pen. It was pitiful, but it was beautiful. I knew he'd walk again. He had guts.

10

MY intermittent love of animals is, I suspect, a trait congenitally acquired from my mother who, during my childhood, experimented with many different kinds of animals—starting on Long Island with rabbits raised for fun and profit. There was no profit, and the rabbits had all the fun. And when it came time to ship the Belgian hares and Dutch Belts and whatever tricky breed she had had on hand to market, Mother had misgivings about the upcoming slaughter of her precious bunnies, and she informed the rabbit dealer that all of the rabbits had died of snuffles, a disease which sounds like a funny bad cold but *is* fatal to rabbits.

This got the rabbit dealer off mother's back, but what now? Dad suggested, "Why the hell don't you just take them out in the woods and let them go?" We were living on Long Island way back when Long Island had trees substituting for Levittown.

"No," Mother said, "they wouldn't know what to do in the woods all by themselves."

"You can teach 'em," Dad said.

"Yeah," said my little brother, "teach em."

Mother looked forlorn, so Dad, who was usually undemonstrative, cracked his reserve and put his arm around Mother. "We'll help you," he said, waving his other arm toward my little brother and me.

"But," Mother said, "we've got eight hundred and sixty-nine rabbits! We can't teach eight hundred and sixty-nine rabbits how to live by themselves out in the woods."

"Why not?" Dad said. "Do they have to have individual instruction?"

"We could leave 'em out in the woods near Old Man Brown's farm—he's got a helluva field of lettuce right next to the woods," I said, knowing all the while I was suggesting something which would get those eight hundred and sixty-nine rabbits bumped off on their very first day of freedom. Old Man Brown was probably the most sensitive man alive when it came to his lousy field of lettuce. He spent all of his waking hours on patrol with a double-barreled shotgun loaded with dumdum bird shot. And when Old Man Brown slept, he had his entire lettuce field booby-trapped, which made it tough on Bernie Maslik, the town drunk, who sometimes took a shortcut across Old Man Brown's lettuce field on his way home from some friendly neighborhood speakeasy. One Labor Day midnight, Bernie lost three toes and part of his left ear—but this didn't stop him from shortcutting across Old Man Brown's lettuce field any night he felt like it. He figured he had seven toes left and almost an ear and a half—so what the hell.

Mother ignored my suggestion, but eventually, weeks later, Mother, Dad, my little brother, and I released nine hundred and thirty-two rabbits into a large woodsy area far from Old Man Brown's lethal lettuce patch. We checked up on them from time to time, and they seemed to be thriving but not nearly as trusting as they once had been.

Mother then ran the gamut: chinchillas, Siamese cats, and experimental mice for Harvard, but Harvard never got the chance to inject them with yellow fever germs or force them to smoke Sweet Caporals—Mother just couldn't bear the thought. She also tried breeding rattlesnakes which were raised for their venom (what else?), which as I dimly remember was used for medicinal purposes by some local laboratory. Or maybe we were living near some mad doctor who was trying to bring Bela Lugosi back to life. Or maybe it was the other way 'round.

All of these animals and reptiles wound up in the woods with the rabbits where, according to my father, they were interbreeding—rattlers with rabbits—bringing forth a whole new species—poison Easter bunnies. My father, who was an Englishman to the nth degree, never changed his expression, so I couldn't tell how much truth there was to his positive statements.

Mother's last animal husbandry hobby before she gave up was the improvement of the breed of German shepherd. This was long before German shepherds were raised to guard used car lots by night and wealthy, but superfluous, little old ladies by day. Mother's dogs were taught to be pets, but somehow they turned out to be ahead of their time and made excellent guards for used car lots and wealthy, but superfluous, little old ladies. Pets they were not. None of us were safe from their inexplicable fury, and the dress of the day was a large, thick, well-padded comforter wrapped around the forearm. These dogs did not attack on command. They based their whole ferocious philosophy on *whim* alone. Some days they were as obsequious as waiters used to be, but without warning they'd switch to the *hounds of hell!*—ripping, tearing, and slashing, and no amount of "Down doggie" would slow them up. This was the first time I realized that there existed a canine organization outside of the American Kennel Club. Mother, without any malice aforethought had brought forth, through careful and selective breeding, a new strain—the German Shepherd Mafia.

The German shepherds could not just be turned loose in the woods, or Long Island would have had to be evacuated. Mother, ever faithful and kind to the end, contracted a wealthy superfluous little old lady who owned a used car lot and made a deal for our entire supply. We hated to see them go because about all the excitement we had left was *Amos and Andy* on the radio and Evelyn and her Magic Violin, who lived next door to us and practiced all day long—nude before an open window. Poor Dad had to go to work, but my little brother and I never missed a performance. My little brother and I became dirty old men before we reached puberty.

Thinking it over, maybe I wasn't so intrigued by animals because of my mother's wild schemes to get rich overnight with some kind of a commercial menagerie. I think it was more curiosity than anything else. The love and compassion came later when I found out what a

51

rotten deal the animal world was getting from we almost-humans.

When I was a boy, which was more years ago than I care to admit—don't you love that phrase? Instead of being proud and happy that we've lived this long we're always *apologizing* for it. *Forgive me, world, but it's not my fault that I've lived this long—it's that goddamn Geritol!* Anyway, when I was a boy, I used to trap muskrats. We lived near a huge swamp which was alive with muskrats, and their skins were sold to some fur dealer in St. Louis (Funsten, I think) for one, two, or three dollars, depending on the texture and color of the fur.

I used to think it was a fun sport to get up at four in the morning and go out into the great swamp and check my traps, and whenever I found a muskrat in one I'd enthusiastically bash him in the head until he was dead, then I'd remove his mangled foot from the steel jaws of the trap, reset the trap, and go on to the next rendezvous with death.

I can't picture myself doing this. Maybe all of us are *born* cruel and learn *not* to be. Whatever it was, I shudder to think of it now, and if there was any way of undoing these terrible deeds, I would do whatever necessary. Today I won't kill an ant knowingly. The swatting of flies I leave to Reiko. I even go further than this. I won't cut down a tree, either. This is how much I believe in the divinity of nature. On the other hand, I hold human life rather cheaply. Not from any lack of compassion or sympathy for the great problems people have but because there are so bloody many of them.

By the year 2058 the world will be so crowded we'll be standing on each other. And God help us if the people on top start to tap dance.

And they *will*.

11

I HAVE been plagued in recent years by "normal" people. They don't understand my concern and interest in wolves. They don't understand to the point where they inquire, in a highly superior tone, "Are you still saving the wolves?" When I say yes, they bathe me in an indulgent smile and pass quickly on to someone more of *this* world. They get away from me as quickly as possible because I am definitely a little "queer" in the passé meaning of the word. I am just one step away from being wrapped in a wet sheet and given shock treatments because I am troubled more by what is happening in North America than in sending food to the Upper Volta pygmies, or the Biafrans, or the Parkinsons —who live in a development about three miles from us. I *do* send *them* food because they spend their entire income on color TV's. They have a twenty-three-inch set in every room in the house and one in the garage. They haven't missed a rerun of *Perry Mason* in six years.

City people, of course, are completely indifferent to the value of any animal with the exception of man's best friend, and having a dog in the city seems to be some sort of status symbol, or maybe it goes a little deeper. It could be that having a dog reveals, more positively than any other manifestation, the great loneliness urban living instills in the psyche of the city dweller. I had a dog when I was a bachelor in New York. His name was Baby—a full-grown malamute I had bought from a retiring dogsled driver one drunken night when Bonnie and the Three Clydes were playing a gig in Moosejaw, Saskatchewan. Little did I know what I was getting into. This poor dog had never been out of the woods before. He had never seen a hotel, a taxicab, an elevator, or anything else so frightening. As a consequence, I had to carry his hundred-plus pounds into taxicabs, hotels, elevators, and everywhere else that looked scary to him. He wouldn't eat or have a bowel movement anywhere but in the center of Central Park at two in the morning.

There was no danger of muggers or anything else in Central Park then, but in the middle of winter you could freeze solid and not be found until spring. The ritual of taking Baby out into the middle of the park night after snowy, icy night palled in a short time. I not only had to take him to the park, I had to get down on my knees in deep snowdrifts and beg him to "eat the nice hamburger Daddy bought," and then after what seemed hours, I had to entreat him to empty his bowels before he burst so we could go home to the Dixie Hotel and get some sleep. I even demonstrated *how* it was done. Try *that* on a below-zero night in Central Park!

After some weeks of this nightly Polar expedition, I gave up. I decided I'd rather be lonely. Baby was eating all right, but to find *just* the right place to "take a dump," as we used to say at Harvard, took hours. *Why* dogs have to spend eons searching for just the right location for their overdue voidance I have never been able to learn. It's not like an animal staking-out-a-territory thing by urinating checkpoints on the boundary lines. *This* I *can* understand. I do it myself. This not only saves me a surveyor's fee but, as our friendly neighborhood exhibitionist has often said—to the arresting officer —"A little of God's sunshine never hurt *anything.*"

W.C. Fields, a bygone philosopher second only to Plato and Moms Mabley, once said that "anyone who hates children and dogs can't be all bad," which was a very funny observation (at the time). He may have been onto something. We all love children—*our* children—and most of us love dogs, but what good are they? True, a dog may be very handy at rounding up stray sheep, but how many of us have stray sheep or the urge to round them up? A great minority.

Children are a different story. They're no help at all when it comes to stray sheep, or anything else. Up until the age of three they are adorable and cute and cuddly and return tenfold the love you lavish all over them. Soon after this comes nursery school, where they start their years of discontent. First it's the kid who had more toy cars than they have. Then it's the kid who has a better bike—or if not better, a different kind of "sissy bar" on it than your kid has. This makes your kid very unhappy—especially with *you*. You don't give him the things that other kids have, therefore you're a sonofabitching bastard (this is their language—not mine) of a parent. Instead of holding the kid's head under water until he stops struggling, which is what you want to do, you rush right out and buy the biggest and bestest sissy bar that ever existed. It's platinum and covered with diamonds, rubies, and emeralds. Your kid now thinks you're super, for at least a day—or until he sees another kid who not only has a jewel-encrusted sissy bar but it's attached to a gorgeous minibike! Right away you are back to the sonofabitching bastard designation until you come across with a minibike. Plus a three-toned klaxon horn which plays the idiotic *Sesame Street* theme song loud and clear.

Our children, Bobby and Timothy, are going to grow up loving their parents (even if they don't have the best sissy bars in town), because I tell them if they don't love us I'll beat them both with a rawhide strap—soaked in salt and vinegar (it *really* smarts). This makes them love us.

Children enjoy discipline, even if it's dished out by a disciple of the Marquis de Sade. So far Bobby and Timothy adore Reiko and me. They flinch a lot, but they adore us.

All this is leading up to (I think) the reason for my penchant for wild animals, specifically wolves. Wolves have always held a fascination for me—as they have had for man since time began. Wolves have always been feared—wrongly so, but feared—and fear, of course, has great attraction for most people. Otherwise why would we have roller coasters, downhill skiing, high-speed auto racing, and marriage?

My first wolf—my beloved Tanuki, who died in frenzied terror when I forced him into a travel crate for a trip to California—came from John and Sandra Harris in California. John and Sandra live across the bay from San Francisco and raise wolves. The wolves they raise are placed in groups in areas from which the wolf had long ago been extirpated and which now have been designated (a little late) as game refuges.

They have had some success in this most worthy project, but not without the trials and tribulations which any progressive ideology experiences, if it has merit. John Harris has served innumerable thirty-day jail sentences for contempt of court. He has steadfastly refused to remove his wolf breeding preserve from Alameda County for many reasons; his wolf kennel is far from any residential community, located as it is in a strictly manufacturing area, where the howl of a wolf, or a *pack* of wolves, cannot be heard above the grinding cacophony of the forces of progress. The Harrises' lupine ménage is constructed of solid concrete and steel-fenced, escape-proof pens and is immaculate—so why aren't the Harrises left alone to continue their nonprofit (*and how*) project? I'm not sure I know, but apparently some county official with an overly stimulated pragmatical gland and a lot of time on his hands decided they must take their wolf kingdom and get the hell out. John Harris thinks otherwise. And despite the clout of San Francisco newsmen like Herb Caen who crusade valiantly on the side of the Harrises, John still serves an occasional thirty-day contempt term in the county jail. And he's starting to talk like Richard Widmark.

12

THE house we have in Honansville was built in 1769 and had been, at one time, a tavern and a stagecoach stop. This gave us something in common with every other ancient house in Honansville. They *all* had been at one time a tavern and a stagecoach stop.

Either the now-owners of these old houses are liars, or Honansville at one period in its history had been the tavern and stagecoach capital of the world. And how Washington ever got his troops out of all those taverns and back into marching formation after an overnight stop in Honansville is more than ample proof of what a great military leader he was. He had to be a military *genius*.

Our Honansville home may not have been built in 1769, but in looking over some of the old deeds filed at the Honansville town hall and the historic records cataloged by the Honansville Historical Society, it *was* very old and had been built by a Honansville iron mine tycoon by the name of Ezekiel Pettibone, who apparently was also in the stagecoach and tavern business, and we were satisfied, more or less, that it was somewhere near as venerable as the real-estate man said it was. In the yellowed records concerning old Pettibone's place, all the *S*'s were written like *F*'s and the house was equipped with "Indian shutters." When I asked the real-estate man, who was new in Honansville, what the hell the "Indian shutters" were used for back in those Colonial days, he said, "I think when the Indians attacked, the people used to close the Indian shutters for privacy."

"That sounds logical," I said.

"Not to me," he said. But it is a lovely old house. And tall, too. It has three floors and an attic. We loved the place and so did Wolf. I'm sure he thought we bought it just for him—to chew on. There were wolf teeth marks on every newel post of every flight of stairs from the basement to the attic, and on every hand-carved mantelpiece over each of our seven smoky fireplaces. There wasn't a door that hadn't been raked and severely loosened from its hinges, and in one case ripped completely from its jamb. This was the kitchen door, which Wolf either resented being closed and off limits to all wolves at all times, or maybe it was just easier prey because its screws were loose. Nevertheless, I came upon him early one afternoon busily reducing it to salivated sawdust. Or trying to. I attempted to soft-talk and reason, but nothing happened, and I knew better than to try to take it away from him. There's an old rule concerning situations like this, the curator of the Bronx Zoo once told me: "Never try to take a kitchen door away from a full-grown timber wolf!" This seemed like good advice. So I left him snarling with a mouth full of golden oak splinters and went to the den—*my den*—to watch our prolific television set. Wolf, suddenly losing interest in the kitchen door when he found that I wasn't going to make a stink over it, got to his feet, coughed, and followed me. Then as I sat down in my easy chair, he threw himself at my feet and immediately fell asleep. I thought then how childlike a wolf is—or maybe it should be how wolflike a child is.

With Wolf, who now was approaching his full growth and looked enormous, lying at my feet, I tried to find out what was on the tube, and as usual it was a montage of four programs at once. We have only one set, but in the hills where we live every channel comes in clearly—if you have a disordered mind or don't mind watching football, hockey, the weather report, and *Nanny and the Professor* at the same time. You may never find out who's playing or who wins or how bad the hurricane is going to be or whether *Nanny and the Professor* is about a Harvard dean who screws goats, but it's better than nothing. At least it keeps you from thinking. It's like having a lobotomy vicariously. I dozed.

Suddenly, from far above, Reiko screamed like she'd just been grabbed by Leopold and Loeb and Sacco and Vanzetti and Pearl Bailey. For ten years she had been telling me that she never had *screamed* about anything in her life. Well, she must have been practicing secretly, because this was the most blood-chilling banshee wail I've ever heard. I made it all the way from the ground floor to the attic without touching a step.

The screaming didn't stop, and for a moment it didn't sound like Reiko at all; from the direction it could have been God, but then God doesn't have a high voice, from all reports, and he doesn't scream when something annoys him. He just smotes. It had to be Reiko.

It was, and she was screaming again when I got to her, or maybe it was the same scream. By this time

I was screaming, too. On my mad dash across the full length of the attic to where Rieko was anguishing, I hit the top of my skull twenty-three times on twenty-three low beams, inflicting twenty-three extremely evenly spaced fractures and sounding like Tom Sawyer rattling a stick along Becky Thatcher's picket fence.

"What the hell's the matter?????" I managed to scream before I swooned.

"A mouse!!!!!!" Reiko screamed back, standing there with a vacuum cleaner, which she had been using to redistribute the dust in the attic.

"Jesus Christ!" Bobby, who had just arrived at the disaster area, said. "A *mouse*?????????"

"What did he do," I asked—postponing my swoon—"rape you?"

"He's here in the attic!" Rieko said, toning down somewhat.

"My God," I said, "he'll die if we don't get him *out* of here!"

"What?" Reiko said, amazed (I think).

"Yeah," I said. "He'll get the Black Lung."

"What's that, Papa?" Bobby said.

"It's a thing that coal miners get from all that dust in the air."

"Oh."

Reiko was standing there, frozen with fright and indignation. "Aren't you gonna kill the mouse?" she said.

"I've *never* killed a mouse," I said, "and I'm not going to start in now. I'll catch it and take it outside and let it go."

"It'll come right back here!" Reiko said.

"We'll buy a cat," I said.

"We got a mountain lion, Papa," Bobby said, ever on his toes. "What do we need a cat for?"

"That's an idea," I said. "We'll put Pussycat up here and give her a contract on the mouse."

"What's that?" Bobby wanted to know.

"That's what Efrem Zimbalist, Jr., says every Sunday night on the FBI program," I said. "It means like a hired killer—you pay somebody to kill somebody else."

59

"That's cool," Bobby said, choosing his words carefully. "What are you gonna pay Pussycat?"

"Nothing," I said. "She can keep the mouse—that's payment enough."

"There he goes! He's big!" Reiko was screaming again. Bobby and I, in our anxiety to get the hell out of the way of this unseen saber-toothed mouse, had a severe collision which dumped us both on the floor. For at least three minutes we couldn't see anything but the swirlings of the dust bowl. I felt like a 1933 Okie who had died and gone back home. As soon as visibility returned, I instructed Bobby to go fetch a wire-bottomed vegetable strainer.

"What are you going to do," Reiko asked, "strain the mouse?" Reiko can be quite witty sometimes—or more likely, just literal.

"No," I said, with all the patience of a twenty-mule-team driver crossing Death Valley in August. "I'm going to slip it over him and keep him confined. Then I'm going to slip a piece of cardboard between the vegetable strainer and the floor—if I can find it—and then the mouse will be in a little cage, which I will carry outside and release him."

"Gee," Bobby said, arriving breathlessly with the strainer. "Cool! Are you going to teach the mouse how to hunt so he'll be safe in the jungle?" Bobby wanted next to know.

"Why not?" I said. "I'd never forgive myself if I released this mouse into a world he didn't make without at least some knowledge of the law of the jungle."

"*I* know the law of the jungle," Bobby said.

"Oh, really?" I said, in a tone which was meant to discourage but worked just the opposite.

"Yeah," Bobby said. "We learned it in school—in social studies." "Social studies" is now what *we* used to call history in my grammar school days. No wonder the kids don't trust anybody over thirty—*we* didn't have *social studies!*

"We ought to send Bobby out on a lecture tour—I think he's ready." I said to Reiko, who was getting up steam for another burst of hysteria. She was pointing under an old bed, which must have been discarded in 1778—right after Betsy Ross and George Washington slept in it. (I'm *sure* there must have been *something* between those two—*he* wanted the flag with the stripes going *vertically* and *no* stars, just thirteen little cherubs in a circle—kissing each other's rosy-pink buttocks—representing the number, and the refreshing innocence, of the original thirteen newly born states. But it's my guess that Betsy pillow-talked him out of this Botticelli conception of what an American symbolic device should look like; and we should all be grateful that she did, because through the years one cherub would have been added for each additional state, and this would surely further burden our age of discontent. Some group, sooner or later, would demand that some of the rosy-pink buttocked cherubs be *black,* which would ruin Botticelli's whole career. Also with a flag design of fifty cherubs nuzzling each other, it might be nigh impossible to get an all-volunteer army. Of the type volunteer the Pentagon has in mind.

Reiko had gone into shock. All she could do was *point*. Like a bird dog.

"Give me the vegetable strainer," I said to Bobby in the same tone I'm sure Grant used when he asked for Lee's sword. Bobby quickly complied, and I once again moved in on the mouse who, I was hoping, was unaware he was about to be caged and sold down the river to a rich rat who owned a cotton plantation. This is what I told Bobby when he had the temerity to ask what I was going to do with the mouse.

"He *wants* to *know!*" Reiko shrilled. "Don't give him any *phony* answers!"

I was too busy lining up the mouse to think of a snotty reply. I could see him now, under the bed, concentrating on accumulating enough of the fluffy stuff he was combing out of the bottom of the mattress to make a cozy little nest for himself and his family somewhere in *our* cozy little nest. He seemed to be unaware that I was about to pop the vegetable strainer over him, and as he made ready to carry off a bundle of mattress stuffing, I asked Bobby and Reiko to lift the bed a little

61

so I could get under it and have room to swing the strainer.

As Bobby and Reiko did so (without question), the mouse became instantly alert. The vegetable strainer was slowly being positioned over his head when Timothy moved into the attic with his fat little rubber-bellied toy clown which, when squeezed by Timothy—or, I guess, anybody—emitted a loud hee-haw screech; and as Timothy moved into the attic he squeezed his toy clown's belly and it screeched—thus ripping what was left of my frazzled nerves into frizzled shreds. I immediately went to pieces and ran smack into a booby trap. It was a large garden rake, which had been strategically placed by the Vietcong on the floor of the attic and skillfully covered with smoothed over dust. The booby trap worked like a charm—the handle, in a wild fulcrum, rose from its concealing dust and bashed me a giant-killing bash on the frontal area of the already much abused frontal area of my skull. I went down like the *Andrea Doria*. But with no heroic musical group on the afterdeck playing "Nearer, My God, to Thee," with the waves lapping its disappearing stern.

Nothing was lapping my disappearing stern, and the only music I heard was very loud bells playing "Toot Toot, Tootsie, Good-bye." I thought, *this* is *it,* and my whole life flashed in front of me in a split second. That did it. I was *glad* to go.

"Later that evening," as they say in Broadway play programs, I was propped up in bed with a casaba melon on my head, which Reiko was trying to bring down with ice bags and laser beams.

"Papa," Bobby whispered right into my ear, almost causing my cerebellum and my cerebrum to wrap around each other like yin and yang from the concussion. Bobby must have sensed that I was a terminal case, because he said, "I'm goin' outside and play." He slammed the front door on his way out and I heard the bells again. This time they were playing a medley of all of Yoko Ono's hits. At intermission I said to Reiko, who was fretting because she wanted to get back to her rice pot and

other projects that matter in real life—*her* real life—
"What about the mouse in the attic?"

"Let him stay," she said, with a distinct air of practical resignation.

"Let him *stay?*" I *couldn't* believe it. "Let him *stay*
—after all *that*—this *afternoon?*"

"Look," Reiko said, "if we've got a *wolf* living in the
living room, why should we worry about a *mouse* living
in the *attic?*"

13

WOLF, who was increasing in size at an
alarming (to Reiko) rate, still dominated our living
room, but he was becoming more tractable and more
understanding as to what was expected of him. This was
accomplished by much patience on our part and with a
heavy leather slipper wacking him on the nose at increasingly shorter intervals. His nose seemed to be his
sensitive part, but not consistently. There were times
when he had been particularly wolfish about some minor
problem when continued hard raps on the nose didn't
faze him in the least. It was like belting Joe Frazier with
a pig bladder from a very soft pig. But he was learning
that the couch was ours and not his, and that knocking
Timothy down with his tail wasn't being done, and also
all urination must be performed *outside*. I knew we
never would be able to housebreak a wolf completely,
or even come anywhere near this impossible dream, but
if we remembered to take him out frequently we could
save what little there was left to save of our living-room
carpeting.

The living-room carpeting had not been ravaged so
much from wolf wetting as from wolf hunting. He hunted
mice, which he was sure were under the carpeting, by
leaping into the air, then pouncing with his front paws
at any spot in which he suspected mice were lurking.

Then when he was disappointed with the result of his magnificent efforts, he would start to dig the non-existent mouse out of the rug, just as he would do in the matted leaves and grass of the woods.

This created a living-room rug which looked like it had been purchased on the installment plan—and we had missed quite a few payments—with bald spots where the carpeting had been repossessed. One bald spot per missed payment. We got goddamn good and tired of explaining to visitors what had really happened to no avail. They always thought we were just slobs—or dead-beats.

We tried Wolf at mouse hunting in the attic, but his monstrous pounces loosened most of the fragile plaster in the bedrooms below; so this hunting area had to be classed, eventually, as off limits.

Bobby, our oldest, was not as conformable as Wolf, I felt—especially when I would occasionally suggest: "Bobby, would you mind washing your face—your teacher said she might drop by today."

"Supposing she doesn't drop by—then what?"

"Waddya mean—*then* what?"

"I'll be stuck with a clean face!"

I have read every book that was ever written about how to raise children, and still I don't know. I've read Spock, Ginott, and Clyde Beatty, and nothing they ever said relates in any way to my nine-year-old, Bobby. Maybe *that's* why I like to raise wild animals—they're more civilized. They stick to the rules and regulations. Animals are wild, but they aren't weird. A nine-year-old boy is spooky. I don't care what Mrs. Dillinger said, *some* kids are *problems*. But I'm giving the wrong impression. Bobby isn't a problem—he's just a little nine-year-old boy trying to find himself in a world full of unbalanced adults. He wants to grow up fast. He doesn't realize how much better it would be if he remained a nine-year-old boy.

Bobby, who balks at anything resembling a *chore* around the house, adores animals. He won't bring in the firewood except after a thirty-minute debate with me threatening to cut his thumbs off if he doesn't. These threats don't rock him too much because he knows that basically I am a beautiful person. Ugly, but beautiful. But when it comes to animals, Bobby is different. He'll haul food and water for the dogs and the mountain lion and hay for their beds. He'll endure being thrown violently to the ground by mock attack on the part of Pussycat who, when the mood is on her, delights in jumping any moving thing—preferably *Bobby*.

Bobby is not quite sure with the wolf. A wolf's affectionate biting with his Wilkinson-sword-blade teeth would tend to make any aware child suspect that there was more to a wolf than meets the eye. A wolf is not a four-legged Barbie doll.

Nevertheless, Bobby did not back off from Wolf, no matter how rough he got, which was not only admirable in Bobby but the smart thing to do in handling any wild or nondomesticated animal. If you show the least weakness, the animal seems to sense it and will become more aggressive and much harder to control. Many times I had observed Wolf, and also our mountain lion, throw a bluff just to test us. The bluffs sometimes worked because the utter, naked ferocity the animals exhibited looked like the real thing, but after a few experiences with this sort of behavior (during which you have to remain strong and retain the blind faith in your conviction that the beast doesn't really mean it when he springs at you with a heart-stopping, apparently feral malevolence). This takes quite a bit of doing.

Bobby loves the animals, but Reiko has a very low threshold of fauna tolerance. I have almost given up trying to impress upon her that every living thing must be allowed to live, which, as a *Buddhist,* she should *know;* but she blithely goes right on killing spiders, wasps, flies, and mosquitoes, who unsuspectingly wander into the house—not realizing that an assassin waits within.

"A Buddhist doesn't kill *anything,*" I've said to her a million and a half times. "That's your *religion!*"

"What's *your* religion?" she wants to know.

"I'm an Episcopalian," I say every time.

"Does an Episcopalian kill anything?"

"An Episcopalian only kills the thing he loves," I say. "And do you know who I love?"

"You love Mamma," Bobby says.

"Yes," I say, "I love Mamma."

"If you're gonna kill Mamma," Bobby said one day, vigorously socking a baseball home into the pocket of his spit-browned first-baseman's mitt, "would you mind waiting a little while, Papa?"

"Why?" I said.

"Because it's almost lunchtime," Bobby said.

Reiko, poor little thing, has to stand still for this kind of carrying on between Bobby and myself all the time. She doesn't understand what the hell we are talking about and usually starts to vacuum something she had just vacuumed earlier—in self-defense—or to gather her thoughts or her strength in order to combat these crazy Yankees.

Like a fool, I always try to point out to Reiko that in flaunting her religious background and killing the spiders, wasps, flies, and mosquitoes, she is not only upsetting our ecology but doing herself a disservice, because the spiders and the wasps are on our side—they knock off lots of little bugs which are our enemies (presumably)—like moths and termites and so on.

"What about the flies and the mosquitoes?" she wanted to know. "Are *they* good?"

"Let somebody else kill them," I said, ducking this issue. "Then you won't have to take the rap on judgment day."

"What's that?"

"That's when God comes down here and judges everybody to see whether they've been good or bad," Bobby said. "Right, Papa?"

"Yes," I said. "What are you gonna tell him about all those spiders and wasps and flies and mosquitoes you murdered?"

"Yeah, Mommie," Bobby said, now throwing his ball against the wall, bouncing the pictures off their hooks. "What are you gonna say to God?"

"I'm gonna make rice," Reiko said, retreating toward the kitchen and sanctuary.

"Mamma's gonna make rice for God?" Bobby asked.

"It sounded that way, didn't it?"

"Supposing God doesn't like rice?"

"Everybody likes *Mamma's* rice."

"I hope so," Bobby said.

When my first wolf died, I don't think anyone felt it more strongly than Bobby. He tried to comfort me, and I tried to tell him that Tanuki was now in the Happy Hunting Ground, and he was happy because nothing more could ever hurt him or scare him again.

"Is there really a Happy Hunting Ground, Papa?" Bobby said.

"I hope so," I said. "I want to believe there is."

"Why didn't Tanuki go to heaven?" Bobby asked.

"Heaven is segregated," I said, sounding more bitter than I meant to. "Heaven is for people—'good' people." Bobby thought about this for quite a while. Then he said, "Where do you wanna go when you die, Papa?"

"I dunno," I said, "but I want to see Tanuki again."

"So do I," he said, tears welling in his lovely deep-black eyes. "So do I—I loved Tanuki so much. So very, very much."

I didn't have much luck in holding back my own tears as I put my arms around my little boy and held him tight. "We'll see him," I said. "We'll see him."

We will, too.

14

QUITE a few years ago when I lived in California, I bought a lovely 320-acre ranch for what was considered a lot of money then. Today, for the same amount of money I paid for the whole 320 acres you can't buy a 50-foot lot, even if you are lucky enough to run into a seller who is an actor who didn't quite make it in TV, porno movies, or the Milk of Magnesia commercials.

This ranch was up in the hills above and off Topanga Canyon. It was not only beautiful, it was unusual—with Indian pictographs in its numerous small caves—and it came with a *live buffalo!* I think I bought the place because of this. I *know* this is the reason I bought it. The buffalo was the lone survivor of a herd of twenty, which some previous owner had raised to give this beautiful ranch the flavor of the Old West. I don't know what happened to the other nineteen buffalo, but I know what happened to mine—some kid shot it with a .22. I was corraled just in time by a sheriff's posse and disarmed as I was storming toward the house where the kid lived.

Nothing much happened to the kid in the way of punishment because he was under sixteen. Later, when they caught this same kid raping his schoolteacher just after he set her hair on fire (because he was afraid of the dark), he was *still* under sixteen so the judge let him off with a reprimand and he couldn't listen to *Amos and Andy* for *two whole weeks!* After a while, I remembered that "to *err* is human," so I forgave him for shooting my buffalo, but through the years I've often wondered what happened to little Charlie Manson. He probably turned out just fine.

The buffalo episode soured me on the ranch, which was a pity because I've never seen anything since as breathtaking, with its meadows, streams, and huge jutting boulders and its cosy ranch house nestled in a grove of pine trees planted fifty or so years before. I sold it to the first buyer who came along, and I'm sure it is now a conglomerate of shopping centers patronized by thousands upon thousands of new Californians looking for Colonel Sanders.

I mention this senseless buffalo killing to point up the problem of owning any *wild* animal. Or any animal, for that matter. How many cows, horses, and other livestock are shot (purposely) by hunters? (And how many hunters are shot by hunters? Not enough, to my way of thinking, but that is another thought entirely.) A hunter with an empty game sack—or a congenital frustration (which most of them have)—will shoot at anything!

Even inanimate objects, such as street signs, lights, or a little old lady sitting in her favorite rocker near a window with her *Reader's Digest*. She's just *asking* for it during deer season.

With my animals I'm always very careful to see that they don't get any ideas about escaping, and so far as I have observed, wild animals born in captivity have no wish to escape. Most animals dig holes; but our wolf never dug along the *edges* of his pen as he would if he were planning a dash for liberty. When he used his powerful front paws with their immense toe spread to gouge out a mild depression, it was usually near the center of his pen. His main object seemed to be the excavation of some huge stone, and he most always succeeded. The strength of this animal was phenomenal. Stones weighing ninety or more pounds were maneuvered, albeit slowly, like a medicine ball in a septuagenarian nudist camp, around his pen.

This does not mean that I believe that any caged animal is completely contented and happy with its confinement. There must be in the minds of most of them, however unformed, the *thought* of freedom. It's very hard, or almost impossible, to sense this quiet desperation, but I know it's there. And they know it's there.

Wild animals who escape, of course, are doomed—the same as a domestic steer who breaks from the herd and makes a dash for it just as he is being driven into the slaughterhouse. Some hero usually guns down this helpless creature before he can "hurt" somebody. A long-horned steer, even if it were dashing through Times Square at high noon, would be of *no actual menace* and, further, nobody would *notice,* except maybe a near-sighted hooker who might mistake him for a newly arrived Viking with a few krona jingling in his pocket and ask, "Wanna have a good time, Leif?"

15

SOME animals who escape, either by accident or design, have been lucky. Ridgefield, Connecticut, which is some distance from Honansville, was the scene last year of a rather bizarre happening involving a resident of Ridgefield who had a well-deserved reputation for being a drinking man—so much so that he had won an Oscar, an Emmy, and a Tony, all presented to him by another Ridgefield resident, an old, rich actor who also hit the bottle.

The beginning of this happening (for me) was a wild midnight call from my friend Dr. Dann, who lives in Ridgefield and is very enthusiastic and protective about animals.

"Jack, has your mountain lion escaped?" Dr. Dann asked, his voice full of trepidation and concern. Dr. Dann is unique—he is a veterinarian who *likes* animals.

"Doctor," I said, "I've been asleep for three hours— I get up at a quarter to four every morning—I need my rest!" I was about to hang up when he said, "There's a guy down here who got picked up by the police for being drunk—but he's also scared, almost in shock! He says he saw a mountain lion. It chased him up a tree."

"Wait a minute," I said, fumbling for my flashlight so I could find my night-light switch. "Some drunk was chased up a tree by a mountain lion?"

"That's what he claims."

"How did the drunk manage to climb a tree—did they give him a sobriety test, make him blow up the balloon?"

"No, he was too drunk for that, but the cops said he could *sure* climb a tree. They took him out and *tried* him."

After checking on Pussycat, my mountain lion, I called

Dr. Dann back and told him Pussycat was safe in her pen.

"Christ, Jack!" Dr. Dann said. "Don't you know what time it is? Look—a doctor's gotta get up goddamn early in the morning. You woke me up just to tell me that your mountain lion is safe in her pen? *Who cares????*"

"*You* do!" I said. "You called me twenty minutes ago to ask me if she'd escaped!"

"Oh, yeah," the doctor said. "Well, let's talk about it tomorrow." Then he hung up—rather loudly, I thought.

The same thing happened the next night. Then two nights after that. Then three nights in a row.

"Doctor," I said, finally, "if you are going to call me every midnight to ask me if my mountain lion is safe in her pen, I'll have to revise my whole mode of living. I'll work at night and sleep days."

"Who *else* is concerned about your mountain lion?" Dr. Dann said.

"Well—" I started. But he was right. There *was* no one.

The calls ceased abruptly, and I didn't have to change my mode of life. I could sleep right past midnight and up until my alarm rang at three forty-five. A comforting thought. Then after about two weeks, the telephone rang. It was way after midnight.

"Doctor," I said, lifting the phone from its cradle, "how nice to hear from you again."

"Jack," Dr. Dann said, "have you got *more* than *one* mountain lion now?"

"What?"

"A huge male—besides the female—and three tiny spotted baby mountain lions?" I assured the doctor that I only had Pussycat, and she had no husband and no baby mountain lions.

"Jesus Christ!" Dr. Dann said. "The drunk was sober tonight and that's what he saw—a male, a female, and three baby lions."

"He was *sober?*" I said.

"Yeah."

71

"Did this squadron of mountain lions chase him up a tree?" I said, pretty bored with the whole thing.

"No," Dr. Dann said, they followed him home and into his kitchen."

I took a deep breath. "Where are they now?"

"In his kitchen," we both said at the same time.

"Wait a minute, Jack, there's someone at the door— I'll call you back," Dr. Dann said. I picked up my copy of St. Nicholas and turned on my reading light. I had gotten no farther than paragraph three of the Anastasia murder case, when the phone ring made me jump three feet straight up.

"Jack," Dr. Dann said, "the mystery is solved."

"You mean Anastasia wasn't murdered after all?" I asked.

"What?"

"Sorry," I said. "I was just improving my mind when you called."

"Well," he repeated, "the mystery is solved."

"Good," I said. "Well, talk to you later."

"Don't you wanna hear what happened?" Dr. Dann said with a pout.

"Yeah, sure I do, Doc," I said. "Why else would I be up at this hour?'

"Well—" he started. "You won't believe this—"

"*Try* me," I said. "*Try* me—I gotta get up and go to work in—"

"Well," Dr. Dann said, quickly, "it seems that there's a guy right here in Ridgefield who secretly raises mountain lions and—" I didn't hear the rest of it—my alarm clock was ringing too loudly.

16

STRANGE about Wolf—as wary and suspicious as he was with an adult human, he was fascinated with a child, or children. It didn't matter how many, which was so contrary to his behavior with large groups of adults who occasionally crowded around his pen. At these times, Wolf would literally climb the walls to get away from them. Then when he realized how futile his attempts at escape were, he'd back off into the farthest corner and stare at the interlopers—his amber-green eyes slitted wickedly, projecting the standard wolf image which deliciously thrilled and chilled his visitors. But with children, his whole attitude changed completely. He was delighted to see them. No matter how many crowded around his pen, he showed no fear or distrust, only love. He wriggled and peed and wagged his tail furiously, his sensitive, animated face reflecting the great joy he felt at being surrounded by only children.

The kids seemed to enjoy seeing him, too, and some of the younger ones wriggled and peed right along with Wolf.

When Wolf started to attain his immense strength and full growth, I had to restrain him somewhat when we brought him into the house—especially when he wanted to romp with Bobby or Timothy. Bobby withstood most of Wolf's outgoing personality a lot better than Timothy, because he knew he must brace himself against Wolf's backside, which he would throw around unexpectedly—like a Dallas Cowboy linebacker clipping from behind. Wolf would clip Bobby, and Bobby would go down. This didn't bother Bobby, because he had reached the age of roughhouse, but with Timothy it was different. Wolf never distinguished between him and his brother, and the same rear-end bump that would knock Bobby down would send Timothy flying through the air. And into the protective arms of his mother, who would immediately demand that Wolf be removed from the living-room and taken out to his wolf pen where he belonged. To Reiko, Wolf was a wolf. She didn't realize that deep inside every wolf is a Dale Carnegie struggling to get out. I don't know what kind of antiwolf fairy tales they scare their kids with in Japan, but Reiko knows that wolves definitely devour little children.

"How come he has never devoured Timothy?" I asked her one day.

"You feed him too much," she said. "He's not hungry enough for Timothy."

"Supposing I don't feed him for a couple of days, then put Timothy in the wolf pen with him and see what happens?" I said.

"I think I go back to Japan," Reiko said, which meant the end of our tête-à-tête about our gourmet wolf. Reiko has three ways of terminating a conversation: She either says, "I think I go back to Japan," or she starts to vacuum, or she cooks rice. Sometimes she cooks rice and vacuums at the same time. This takes dexterity and timing, but she does it well. *I* terminate conversations by storming out of the house and heading back to Canada, but I never get much farther than Joe's Bar and Grill and Bar, which takes the place of a Christian Science reading room in Honansville. After three double martinis I still want to go to Canada, but I forget which numbers to push on my antidrunk driving computer. If I'm not too confused, I can usually punch out the right combination for backing up, but this isn't really practical—my neck gets stiff around Albany.

As time progressed *I* decided that Wolf was a little too rough to have Timothy as a blood brother for a while yet, and a relative peace was restored.

Tranquillity has a transitory quality in our household, and it wasn't too long before World War III, IV, and V broke out.

"Papa?" Bobby said one day as he came panting home from the long run from the school bus stop, "have we got any pets?"

"No," I said, in my endearing Mr. Chips tone. "No, all we have is two dogs, a mountain lion, and a wolf."

"You don't understand, Papa," Bobby said, and he's right—I haven't *ever* understood any kid over three years old.

"What do you mean?"

"I mean—have we got a pet I could bring to school for the pet show?"

"You stay away from that wolf!" Reiko interjected, just before she threw the vacuum cleaner into high gear and started her hill climb up the front stairs.

"What kind of pets are the other kids bringing?" I asked Bobby, trying to ignore Reiko's practice run for the Pike's Peak Grand Prix.

"Oh, all kinds—cats, dogs, raccoons, horses, ponies, calves, sheep, ducks, canaries—you know, all kinds."

"But those are mostly all domesticated animals," I said.

"What do you mean—*domesticated?*" he said.

"Like me." I couldn't resist.

"Can't I bring Pussycat to the pet show?"

"Bring a mountain lion to a kid's pet show at the school?" I said. "Are you nuts?!"

"That's beside the point," Bobby said. "Look, Papa, what will the other kids think if I *don't* bring the mountain lion?"

"Well," I said, "if you put it that way—"

"Then I can?" he said, his beautiful little face brightening with an eager smile.

"No."

There was a sad silence, then Bobby said, "Papa, you're *some* father, *you* are!"

"What's that mean?"

"Other kids' fathers would have said yes."

"How many kids in that school have fathers who have mountain lions?" I asked.

"I dunno," Bobby said, ready to disinherit me from the $25 U.S. Savings Bond he got the day he was born from the little girl in the next incubator (this was the story we'd told him as sort of a buildup to more realistic stories about money and the opposite sex).

"Why don't you take the wolf to the pet show," I said. "Pussycat's too hard to handle, and she might grab a lamb, or a chicken—or a teacher."

"Can I?"

"Sure," I said, "but *I'll* have to bring him because he's not too fond of crowds, and he may be scared."

"Maybe he'll grab a teacher," Bobby said.

"If he does," I said, "make it that cute little blonde with the big knockers who thinks she's teaching you geography."

"Huh?" Bobby said.

75

The pet show started out innocently enough, with a plethora of cats and dogs and baby turtles—the kind which the Connecticut medical authority has been trying to get banned from the state because of botulism, or some such highly potent disease, which produces a rash or fits (it seems you have a choice). The schoolyard at the Old Bridge Street School was jam-packed with pets, parents, and kids, all fondling each other's contribution to the pet show. There were sheep, lambs, three full-sized cows, six Indian ponies, and a swaybacked ancient riding horse whose spine must have been mostly old rubber bands. He looked like a camel with a reverse hump. Some children had pet raccoons, squirrels, and chipmunks, while other not so fortunate children, evidently from "straight" homes, had gerbils, gerbils, and more gerbils, which I always felt was a polite name for rats.

People who would run right out and buy twenty-five pounds of mint-flavored arsenic if they saw a rat get down on their hands and knees and talk baby talk to a gerbil. There was at least half the gerbil population of the United States right there in the Old Bridge Street schoolyard.

The children of the Old Bridge Street School were dressed at their worst, which was usual, but the parents, outside of a few defiantly nonconforming city folks, were costumed as if they had been invited to share the Royal Box at Ascot. The women all wore large red-polka-dot floppy hats, usually pictured in the society pages on the head of a plump matron standing in a rose garden with a trowel in one begloved hand and a minuscule watering can in the other, the caption reading: "Mrs. Price-House-Water-Finchley-Dutton-Hutton-Copley-Plaza-Jones pruning her prize roses" (they never explain *how* she does all this pruning with a trowel and watering can). The rest of the garmenture, apparently *de rigueur* for schoolyard pet shows, were largely filmy flowered things made from a blueprint of the original Hawaiian muumuu, dainty slippers, and sheer pastel-blue, pink, or chartreuse pantyhose. This is a surmise on my part, but I felt that they must be wearing *something* on this order underneath,

76

plus the obvious U.S. Steel I-beam reinforced girdle.

There were very few fathers in sight at the Old Bridge Street School pet show, presumably because they were at work—or hiding in the hills.

The hit of the pet show (before Wolf arrived) was a pet Indian myna bird, who had a two-word vocabulary and a fanatic desire to be heard. Loud and clear. The two words in his vocabulary were "Peace!" and "Shit!" And his pronunciation and enunciation were perfect. As a pet at a grammar school pet show his rating was "X." Nevertheless, he was allowed to stay because some of the mothers felt that his message was half right. *Which* half depended on how long the mother had been hanging around the Old Bridge Street School pet show on this broiling September day.

By lunchtime, most of the loyal but suffering parents had had it with the Old Bridge Street School pet show and enough of proud, innocent little children shoving gerbils into their faces to be kissed. "Christ!" someone said, under his breath, "if you've kissed one gerbil you've kissed them all!"

I arrived in our station wagon a little after twelve noon. I had intended to be there at ten, but Wolf had other ideas than getting into a station wagon. He braced himself against every tree, bush, and blade of grass, plus a few deeply embedded rocks, which made excellent footing for his last stand against my mighty heaves on the heavy chain leash with its two choke collars. Finally, with little Reiko adding her immense rice-nourished strength to shoving Wolf's buttocks, we got him into the wagon and slammed the door. Now all I had to do was drive to the Old Bridge Street School pet show with a spooked wolf jumping from seat to seat to cargo space and back again, all the while slashing at the genuine polyethylene Zebra hide upholstery, tearing out its foam rubber bowels—which is an untidy dissection at best. But with almost surgical skill, Wolf managed to transform the whole interior of what had been a dull, proletarian station wagon into a fairyland of foam rubber fuzz.

The seven-mile drive to the Old Bridge Street School

was a nightmare to be remembered. Wolf hadn't ridden in the station wagon enough not to be frightened witless by every tree, every farmhouse, every parked pickup truck, every strange leaf that fluttered down from a breeze-tickled oak. He'd never seen so many strange leaves before, and he reacted violently to *every one* of them. He alternated between crouching behind the back seat to trying to make himself invisible on my lap. Having a 150-pound wolf in your lap while driving a car down a twisting, narrow mountain road can change your whole attitude toward life. Suddenly it becomes very precious—because something tells you there isn't much of it left as you approach the Lovers' Leap curve and you can't reach the brake pedal and a wolf's back feet are standing on the accelerator. I could see the headlines: FAMOUS WRITER DIES IN CAR CRASH—WOLF DRIVING. But, alas, this happy headline was to be postponed, because at the very last Pearl White minute Wolf decided he liked behind the seat better, and I was able to reach the brake and avoid both the Lovers' Leap drop-off and an eighty-year-old man plunging uphill on the left side of the road on a Honda. He gave me the "peace" sign as he neatly veered around me and neatly crashed into a ninety-year-old man on a Yamaha coming *down* the hill. The old man coming down the hill didn't have time to give the full "peace" sign to the old man coming up the hill—he only got as far as raising *one* finger. I can't verify the ages of these people, but I'm pretty close. Also, I couldn't stop and help them because I dared not open my car door. And, besides, motorbikes drove Wolf into a frenzy, and I didn't want to add a bonus to the frenzy he already had worked into an unbelievable pitch. Finally, as we drove the last mile or so to the school, he calmed down. Or he fainted. I was afraid to hope.

We drove through the gates of the schoolyard, having made advance arrangements to have someone open them for us because, as they understood. I couldn't let Wolf run loose among the more standardized type of pet. The gerbils might all drop dead. Or try to kiss him.

When Bobby, already waiting there for me and Wolf,

spotted us he let out a whoop and screamed, "There's my wolf! There's my wolf! There's my wolf!" This caused quite a few—or almost everybody—in the schoolyard to gather around the station wagon. I nudged Wolf into standing up and acting like a wolf, which he did quite willingly when he saw nothing but small children. But the small children were not impressed. Even when I held up a small sign which read WOLF, they had their doubts. From what I could hear, they didn't believe the wolf, or Bobby. They thought we were pulling a fast one and trying to unload a German shepherd dog on them as a wolf. I could hear Bobby desperately trying to convince them as they drifted back to their bunny rabbits and their chipmunks and their gerbils. "It *is* a wolf!" he yelled tearfully. "It *is!* It *is! IT IS!*"

I couldn't really condemn any of them for doubting Wolf's authenticity, because so little is known about wolves and none of the children knew exactly what a real wolf was supposed to look like.

Bobby's tears led me to drop my guard for a moment and open the car door to comfort him. In that instant Wolf was out of the car and running free in the schoolyard. There was utter panic, with screams, "The wolf! The wolf! The wolf is loose!" Suddenly, the German shepherd had done a Jekyll and Hyde and turned into a wolf!

Bobby was ecstatic! At *last* they believed him! And *how* they believed him! They were huddled in tight little knots in every possible neutral corner they could find. Mothers stood in half circles in front of their children like arctic musk oxen ready to die defending their calves.

Wolf was running from group to paralyzed group, wagging his tail and wriggling at the children. One poor little girl dropped her gerbil, and the frightened animal ran right in front of Wolf. He ignored it completely and tried to make friends with the little girl who had leaped out from in back of her mother's ample musk oxen behind to recover it. The little girl screamed. As Wolf stopped short at this, she stopped screaming. She gave Wolf a cookie. A Fig Newton, which he'd never had before, and he had trouble with it sticking to his enormous canine teeth. In his efforts to loosen it, his teeth were so prominently displayed that everyone gasped, wondering how many mouthfuls the little girl would make for a hungry wolf.

The little girl gave Wolf another Fig Newton, which he ate with a little more finesse this time. Then she gave him another. I saw salvation in this little girl and her Fig Newtons. I called to her to get in the car and bring her Fig Newtons with her.

"No," she said. "My Mommie said I should not ever get into a car with a strange man."

Holy Christ! I thought to myself, a religious fanatic! But I said, "It's all right, I'm not a strange man."

"Wanna bet?" some Women's Lib disciple yelled.

"Well," I said, "if you don't want to get into the car with your Fig Newtons, just give me your Fig Newtons and you won't have to."

"No," the little girl, who I could see was going to be a problem said. "My mother said I should never give my Fig Newtons to a strange man in a car."

"If I give you a dollar, will you give me your Fig Newtons?" I asked, desperate. The little girl looked over toward her mother—then she turned to me and said, *"Two* dollars." What could I do? I paid the two dollars and lured Wolf back into the station wagon with the Fig Newtons and slammed the door and started to drive away. So far as I was concerned, the Old Bridge Street School pet show was over.

As I passed the little Fig Newton girl, I opened my car window a couple of inches and said to her mother, "What are you gonna do with the two dollars?"

"Buy some more Fig Newtons and wait for the next pet show," she said.

17

"WHAT have you got against children?" asked Dr. David Shimkin as we were riding his horses over the shining green hills of Connecticut. Dr. David Shimkin is an anthropologist, a naturalist, an MD and also a neighbor, who had spent a year in his youth studying wolves and wolf behavior in Canada's Northwest Territories and was pretty much of an authority on the subject. And on many other subjects, upon which we disagreed almost unanimously—which was the basic and quite solid foundation of our friendship. It had seemed, in the five or six years I had known Dr. Shimkin, that whatever *I* believed, *he* believed just the opposite—purposely.

"I have nothing against children," I said. "I'm against the exploiters. The big organizers who skim off the cream of every nonprofit organization and leave the children the curds and whey!"

"But there *must* be an organization," Dr. Shimkin said, "or those Australian bush kids would have to do without hot lunches entirely!" I looked at Dr. Shimkin to see if this was a big put on, but apparently he was playing it straight.

"And," Dr. Shimkin continued, "I like that 'curds and whey' phrase—makes you sound like you know what you're talking about."

"That's another thing," I said, ignoring his cream-puff insult.

"That 'hot-lunch' crap! And I don't mean in the Australian bush—I mean right here in Honansville! That goddamn Old Bridge Street School spends a fortune to feed a lot of kids who would enjoy it a lot more if they could bring their own lunches to school and not have to drive their parents crazy deciding whether or not they like the cafeteria menu for that day or not!"

"You think so?" Dr. Shimkin said, urging his horse next to mine.

"Yes, I do," I said. "Whether *you* think so or not, a lot of kids don't like goddamn filet mignon à la béarnaise, or *coq au vin,* or baked Alaska, or cherries jubilee and espresso *à la napolitaine.* They'd much rather bring a jelly sandwich from home so they can exchange it with one of their classmates for a jelly sandwich."

"That's the same thing."

"No, it isn't—not if you're a kid."

We rode on in silence for a while after this, crossing the little covered bridge at West Cornwall and heading up into the lush valleys of the Housatonic State Forest, fording tiny streams and fast-running creeks. Everything looked like New England should look. Neat and tidy—and thrifty.

We pulled up our horses under a huge oak, which I'm sure back in 1779 General Washington had used as a shelter while he conferred with some French general. This seemed to be the story about *every* huge oak in Connecticut. And it may all be true. There were a lot of French generals to confer with—also a few Polish generals and a few German generals. Which was, apparently, why it took so long to win the war: By the time Washington explained to Lafayette, and Lafayette explained to Pulaski, and Pulaski explained to Von Steuben, it was too late to act. The goddamn British had already shot poor Barbara Fritchie's old gray head full of old gray holes. And poor George was running out of huge oaks. I understand just before Yorktown they had taken to meeting under mulberry bushes. This all came to mind as we dismounted and threw ourselves down in the lush green under the tree. We had ridden a long way and I was ready for a lovely little snooze. Maybe it wasn't Barbara Fritchie—it might have been Lillian Gish—or Martha Mitchell.

"I suppose you think we should forget all about those Australian bush kids and save the kangaroos—*you* and your *animal fixation,*" Dr. Shimkin said, lying back on his hands and looking up through the branches at the cloudless sky. Dr. Shimkin, with his anthropologist-naturalist-MD mind, had the tenacity of a summer cold. I didn't want to talk about Australian bush kids forevermore, but it wasn't to be.

"I *like* kangaroos," I said, shooing away a few curious mosquitoes (they had never seen a white man before).

"What about the *bush kids?*" he said.

"I really don't know much about them—all the *National Geographic* ever shows are pictures of them running around bare-assed naked with their little dingleberries waving in the breeze."

"You know *why* they run around bare-assed naked?" Dr. Shimkin asked. I didn't know, but I knew I was destined soon to find out. "Because they have *no clothes!*"

"Oh."

"*No clothes!*" Dr. Shimkin repeated. "And no *food!* Haven't you seen those full-page ads in *Harper's Bazaar* and *The New Yorker?* 'For *three dollars* you can buy *seven hundred* and *fifty dollars'* worth of food for this Australian Bush Child!' Haven't you seen those ads?"

"Yes," I said, just to keep things on a friendly keel. After all, I'd be in a helluva fix if Professor Shimkin suddenly told me I couldn't ride his horse back to Honansville. "I've seen those ads—what kinda food can you get for three dollars that's worth seven fifty? A carload of redwood shavings?"

"How the hell do I know what an Australian bush kid eats?" he said. "He's gotta eat something! And he's gotta have clothes!"

"Oh, come on, Professor," I said, throwing caution to the winds insofar as my transportation back to Honansville was concerned. "*What clothes?* To them, a Spalding jockstrap would be like a Bill Blass suit!"

"I think you're a reactionary," Professor Shimkin said.

"Why?"

"Because anybody who likes kangaroos better than people has got to be." Professor Shimkin could be right, but I never looked at it quite this way. Why the hell can't we have healthy, full stomached, jockstrapped Australian bush kids *and* kangaroos?

"There's something else I've been wanting to ask you," Dr. Shimkin said, lighting a cigarette with his Zippo. Dr. Shimkin was one who advised his patients, constantly, that cigarettes could kill them.

"Why don't you get a mate for that wolf of yours?" he said.

"You mean," I said, fully awake now, "a female wolf?"

"Offhand, I would think so," Dr. Shimkin said, with a trace of tolerance. "Females seem to make the best mates for males, and I've noticed your wolf is getting restless."

"Have you noticed *me?*" I said. *"I'm* getting restless, too."

"Writers are always restless—and dissatisfied. They should never be married," he said, warming to his subject. "They tend to be unfaithful—and morally bankrupt. They are *sexually voracious."* This was good news, I thought, and I enthusiastically agreed with him—for the first time in years.

"Don't be so exuberant," Dr. Shimkin said, "until you take a good look around Honansville. Who are you gonna be sexually voracious with?" This cooled me considerably. He was right. I had never seen any female in Honansville who could turn me even halfway on. The older ones all looked like Ma and Pa Kettle, and the younger ones looked like the Boston Strangler's rejects. My sexual voracity, I immediately realized, would have to be confined to home games only. Which wasn't working out too badly. But I said, "What do you mean, writers tend to be unfaithful?"

"That means they fool around," he said.

"How about doctors?"

"They fool around, too."

I laughed at this. It was so ridiculous. Dr. Shimkin was married to a gorgeous brunette he had met while on an Israel vacation some years before. Her name was Lillian, and besides her beauty she had one other distinction which is hard to be believed: She had never been a sergeant in the Israeli Army. How many nice Jewish girls can say that?

84

When I got home after my day of riding the bumpiest horse in all of Connecticut, I painfully removed my clothes and eased my aching everything into a warm tub which Reiko had thoughtfully provided. Reiko was always thoughtfully providing warm tubs for me, which is sweet, but the temperature of the water she measures by Japanese standards. Which means that if you were a freshly killed chicken plunged into the same water, your feathers would come off in no time. I have no feathers, but these Oriental heat treatments have made my chest completely bald.

After a bit of agonized shrieking, I settled in the tub for a little serious cooking, vowing that I would never ride a horse again. Even if Jackie Kennedy Onassis *begs* me. The hunt is *out!*

Reiko was all tea, massages, and sympathy, which is a nice thing about Japanese girls—they seem to know when a man has pushed his buttocks too far.

"Lillian Shimkin called," Reiko said, as she tried to rub some restoration into my numbed backside. "She said that Dr. Shimkin said you were against jockstraps."

"That's a lie," I said. "I'm one hundred percent *for* jockstraps. In fact, I'm thinking about picketing City Hall with a large sign reading JOCKSTRAP POWER!"

"What's a jockstrap?" Bobby asked.

"It's a bikini with a crotch pocket," I said.

"James Bond has a crotch pocket," Bobby said. This was news.

"What the hell for?" I said.

"That's where he keeps his secret forty-five automatic —in case of emergencies," Bobby said. I didn't pursue this further, but it seemed I had James Bond figured all wrong.

"Bobby, *quiet*," Reiko said to Bobby.

"Bobby, *quiet*," Timothy said to Bobby.

"*Shut up!*" Bobby said to Timothy, and in no time we were well into a typically restful evening at home. The children bickering, the mountain lion rolling a bowling ball, her favorite toy, around the living-room floor. Doggie, the Pomeranian, who had been raised together with Pussycat, the mountain lion, tried to enter into this fun with her but only succeeded in getting knocked flat several times by the thundering ball propelled vigorously by Pussycat's powerful front paws. Bowling is certainly no game for a four-pound Pom.

Reiko added to this pandemonium by a brilliant display of her vacuum cleaner technique. There was no doubt—she was the Mario Andretti of the Hoover.

At the same time Reiko was running her infernal machine between, through, and around my outstretched, aching legs, she was screaming something about Dr. Shimkin telling his wife that I was going to get another wolf, and Reiko, above the din, was not happy about this.

As soon as the typically restful evening at home with the Douglases was winding down and the dear children and all the animals had been caged for the night, Reiko settled down to complaining about how tired she was, and how her ear ached, and how her itch itched, and asking me a host of medical questions about her condition that would have stumped Dr. Menninger and his entire staff because none of *her* symptoms had ever come up before. With Reiko as a patient, Hippocrates would have quit and become a notary public. The oaths would have been different, but he would have been happier.

Somewhere between "this tremendous pain I have in my forehead" and "this arm—I think I broke it," the telephone rang. I answered it.

"Wait a minute, dear," I interrupted Reiko, "it's Dr. Shimkin."

"Ask him about the terrible pain in my head and my broken arm," Reiko said.

"Okay," I said. "Doctor, what about the terrible pain in Reiko's head and her broken arm?"

"What did he say?" Reiko wanted to know.

"Plenty of rest, drink lots of fluids, and call him in the morning," I said.

"Okay," Reiko said, and turned to the Japanese *Reader's Digest*, leaving me free to discuss whatever cause Dr. Shimkin had thought up between the time we parted in that late afternoon and now.

"Jack," he said, "I'm serious about you getting a mate for Wolf—I think it would be very interesting for *you.*"

"What about Reiko?" I said.

"Oh, I wouldn't drop *her,*" Dr. Shimkin said. "After all, she's your wife."

Dr. Shimkin had a way of deliberately scrambling a conversation so he could put his point over—subtly, he thought. "If you raised a family of wolves," he continued, "it would give me a chance to study them closely. I need a lot of material for this paper I'm preparing for the AMA convention in Las Vegas."

"Las Vegas! For a medical convention!"

"Yes," Dr. Shimkin said. "We're going to use some of those gorgeous show girls as models to emphasize the more important parts of the human body."

"Boy," I said. "Doc, you've come a long way from those skid-row, wino cadavers you used to use for that kinda thing."

"Yes," Dr. Shimkin agreed. "Inflation has changed everything." I didn't know what the hell this meant so I just played it safe and agreed.

"There's one thing I don't quite understand," I said. "Why are you doing a paper on wolves for a bunch of physicians?"

"Apparently you are not aware," Dr. Shimkin said, switching into his clenched-teeth, Westchester voice delivery, "but the highly social nature of *Canis lupus*—the wolf—is closely that of our own, perhaps I should say superior to our own, and through them—the wolf packs—we can learn more about ourselves."

"That sounds pretty high and mighty, Doctor," I said.

"It does, doesn't it?" he agreed. "But"—he then resumed his normal enunciation—"you know I have always been fascinated by wolves, and I'd like to know more about them—even if I never write that goddamn paper."

"What about Las Vegas?" I said.

"Anytime you say," he said.

"I meant the AMA convention," I said.

"Oh—that's not for a couple of years yet. Think it over, Jack. Then after you've thought it over, get Wolf a mate—he needs one." Then he hung up, and I walked over and turned on the television set—I wanted the ten-o'clock news. While the set was warming up and the picture was unscrambling itself, Reiko said, *"No more wolves!"*

I just looked innocent—as innocent as a man who was thinking seriously about getting more wolves *could* look.

18

THE monthly meeting of the Honansville Ecology Group was enjoying itself, at *our* house, as usual. The original charter members were all there: Harry Mitchell and his semilovely wife, Ruthie—they were always the first to arrive so as not to miss a drop. Harry needed a little lubrication before he could retell, word for word and endlessly, his story of his experience in Butte, Montana, with a woman of apparently loose morals and her dog. Harry and Ruthie had decided after much soul-searching to come to the aid of the coyote, as their part of this ecologically minded age. They really had no idea that the coyote needed aiding, except that once on their honeymoon trip, which they had spent at a motel in the Hollywood hills, they had heard the yelping cry of the coyote echoing through the canyons, and this gave the whole idea of doing something for this small desert wolf a sweet, nostalgic, and romantic air. They felt that the yelp of the coyote should be preserved for all the honeymooners of the future. I agreed with them, although not for quite the same reason.

Frank and Ethel Krasselt had been very busy in their fight against Ernie Saloks, who had been just as busy fighting back and, at the same time, gouging sand and gravel out of hills for miles around and filling in swamps and swampy areas much needed for wildlife's sake.

"The cattail is holding its own," Frank and Ethel reported, "and the redwing still has a place to sit, but how long it will last we don't know."

"One of Ernie Saloks' big gravel trucks smacked into a school bus the other day on the South Kent Road," Harry Mitchell said. "That oughta make quite a few points for the cattails and redwings—people don't seem to get very excited about the redwings, but they'll call out the vigilantes if anybody smacks a school bus."

"I think there are too many school buses," Virgil Palmquist said. "Don't you, Reggie?" to his antique shop partner, Reggie Mailer.

"Yes," Reggie agreed, "especially when you're in a hurry. You get behind a goddamn school bus and you are there for *days!* They stop and let the kids out one at a time—every thirteen feet! Whatever happened to *walking* to school? *I* walked to school and it didn't hurt me!"

"I'll bet you got lotsa laughs," Harry Mitchell said, deep in his third martini.

"What's *that* mean!?" Reggie wanted to know. I did, too.

"Because you walk funny!" Harry Mitchell said. Then he half sniggered and half burped, sounding like a minibike stalling out on a hill.

"Oh, go *yelp* with your *coyotes!*" Reggie said, looking down at the disarray that was Harry Mitchell.

Virgil and Reggie's ecology problem was still the preservation of the gray squirrel—*their* gray squirrel—against a mongrel, neighborhood red squirrel. This was not a too important crusade, but they were at least in the right groove for bigger and better causes. And they never missed a meeting.

"School buses cause pollution," Virgil Palmquist persisted. "I don't know what they're burning, but it doesn't seem to be gasoline. There's a foul dark-brown emission pouring out of the rear end of every school bus I've ever been stuck behind."

"I agree with Virgil," Rogers Dotson said. This was a first for Rogers Dotson. He had never before agreed with anybody about anything.

"So do I," Alice Dotson said. "They're smutching up the whole countryside."

89

"Smutching up the whole—?" Harry Mitchell said, pleased that he had caught one of these "high and mighty" Dotsons in a vocabular *faux pas.* "Don't you mean 'smudge,' Alice?"

"If I meant 'smudge,' I would have said 'smudge,'" Alice Dotson said, in *her* clenched-teeth Westchester accent. "I meant 'smutch.' It's a word *you* don't hear every day, Harry Mitchell, but it means the same thing!"

"Well shut mah mouth!" Harry Mitchell said.

"Someday *somebody will!*" Reggie Mailer said.

"Would *you* like to try it?" Harry Mitchell said, setting his king-size martini glass on a well-ringed coffee table and trying to look like a bulldog. I must say, he succeeded.

"Good gracious, no," Reggie Mailer said. "That's a job for a ready-mix cement company. They'd have to make two trips, though." Harry Mitchell now tried to look like a bulldog *and* Edward G. Robinson in *Scarface* before he said, "Oh, yeah!" He didn't look *anything* like Edward G. Robinson.

"Wait a minute!" This from Bella Brown, who sat on a reinforced bar stool next to our tiny corner bar. She was wearing stained jeans and a short-sleeved sweat shirt with a picture of Andre Previn imprinted on the back. She flexed her enormous biceps as she continued. "There's not gonna be any trouble here! If there is, *I'll* start it—and *I'll* finish it!"

"Fair enough," Harry Mitchell said, and terminated his martini in one quick gulp, and immediately headed for the bar and a refill.

"I'd like to say something about pollution," Dr. Shimkin as a new member attending his first meeting of the Honansville Ecology Group, said. "I understand that the Kent School dumps its sewage into the Housatonic River."

"Oh, I wouldn't worry about that," Rogers Dotson said. "It's a very fine school."

Dr. Shimkin was nonplussed at this, and I thought he might have felt some misgivings at becoming a member of this spooked congregation, so I said, "Doctor, what you need is a good stiff drink."

"Jack," the doctor said, "you'd make a great diagnostician. Let's get on with it."

Dr. Shimkin, encouraged immensely by his half tumbler of bourbon, launched into a grandiose speech about what the Honansville Ecology Group must do to save the world—or at least Honansville.

"The first thing we must do is cut down on children," Dr. Shimkin said. "Two should be the limit for every family."

"That's gonna be a problem for us," Frank Krasselt said. "We've got six—which four do we get rid of?"

"Well, now," Dr. Shimkin began. "I didn't mean—"

"I never cared too much about Richard, Philip, Emily, and Phoebe," Ethel Krasselt said. "They were the last four—"

"No, no," Dr. Shimkin said and poured himself another half tumbler as quickly as he could. "If you have children now you should keep them, naturally."

Frank and Ethel looked pretty glum at this news.

"Anybody wanna tea?" Reiko said, again in a desperate and sadly futile attempt to be part of this strange Americana. But, as always, no one wanted tea, and Reiko went back to her gentle silence—wondering where it would end.

Harry Mitchell, taking advantage of a lull in this cross-purposed conversation, said, "Did I ever tell anyone of the ecology problem I ran across in Butte, Montana?"

The newcomer, Dr. Shimkin, before anyone could warn him, said, "An ecology problem in Butte, Montana? Sounds interesting."

Everybody in the room but Harry Mitchell sighed a martyred sigh, as Harry said, "It's a *very* interesting ecology problem. You'll understand right away what the problem was as soon as I tell you." There was a pause while Harry reinforced his will to get loaded in the shortest possible time, and none of us took advantage of this, so Harry continued. "This all happened in Butte, Montana—there was this hooker who had a cocker spaniel, and—"

"It was a St. Bernard," Ruthie, Harry Mitchell's semi-lovely wife, prompted.

"A St. Bernard," Harry said, without missing a beat.

"*I* have a dog story," I said. I just couldn't listen to one more run-through of Harry Mitchell's long-ago, and probably apocryphal, tale of high life in Butte, Montana. And judging from the beatific looks of gratitude on the faces in the rest of the room as I rudely interrupted him, they felt the same way.

"I love dog stories," Alice Dotson said, "especially if they're sad."

"Yes," agreed her husband, Rogers, who sat in my best chair, smoking his poisoned pipe and stroking the imaginary Irish setter at his side. "There's nothing quite so satisfying as a good, sad dog story."

"I like sad horse stories better," Bella Brown said. "I made a pair of shoes today for my oldest mare and I wanna tell you—"

"We're *not interested* in your *oldest mare,* Bella," Virgil Palmquist said, abruptly cutting off Bella in mid-sentence. Bella, who was not used to resistance of any sort, looked hard at Virgil.

"One of these days, Virgil," she said, "I'm going to pull your wings off!"

"May we have the sad dog story now," Alice Dotson said with the great patience and dignity that comes from ninety-proof vodka.

As an apprentice perfect host, I said, "Yes." Then I started, "Once upon a time—"

"Holey Moley!" Harry Mitchell said. "A fairy tale!"

"I hope it's a sad fairy tale," Alice Dotson said, trying to suppress a burst of hiccups.

"There's nothing quite so satisfying as a good, sad fairy tale," Rogers Dotson said.

When all the asides and interruptions for freshening up drinks had subsided, I told them about when Bonnie and the Three Clydes played an engagement at the Dreamland Ballroom in a small town with the unlikely but bona fide name of Maggie's Nipples, Wyoming, and the question of where we were to find overnight accommodations became almost an International Incident. International because Slim Moyston, our piano player, was a Mexican, and Slim insisted on traveling with his pet Great Dane, who was greater than any Great Dane I had ever seen before. He must have weighed 175 pounds dripping wet, which he was most of the time, because Slim, although he didn't go in for water and Dial soap much himself, liked to keep Big Boy, his Great Dane, immaculate. Big Boy didn't smell like a dog. He smelled like Debbie Reynolds.

Maggie's Nipples, Wyoming, didn't offer much in the way of creature comforts, such as a motel with inside plumbing, but it did have a motel. It was called the Maggie's Nipples Hilton, which was a misleading designation, because Snag Hilton, the owner, was connected in no way—either by family or business affiliation—with the owner of the Waldorf-Astoria. Snag Hilton had, by his own bootstraps, pulled himself up into his now exalted position as the largest motel operator in Maggie's Nipples, Wyoming. Albeit, he was the *only* motel operator in Maggie's Nipples, Wyoming, but that was of little import to Snag. "Statistics are crap—with a capital *K!*" was one of his favorite sayings.

Snag was a little taken aback when Slim, whom Snag could tell was *not* from Wyoming, asked if the motel had a policy that excluded dogs. Snag was about to reply that dogs were okay but Mexicans weren't when he remembered that the Maggie's Nipples Hilton hadn't had an occupancy for a month and a half, so he said there was no objection to dogs. Slim then asked to see the accommodations before he signed the register and forked over the four dollars Snag was asking for the "De Lux" cottage. Snag almost lost it at this, but somehow he pulled himself together and handed the "Spick" the key to cottage number three.

Bonnie, Bennie, and I sighed a large sigh of relief at this peaceful conclusion of the negotiations (unless Slim didn't like what he saw) and signed the register. I signed "Mr. and Mrs. Birdsong" for Bonnie and me, while Bennie the banjo player piano picked his nose and scratched his crotch because it was his turn to sleep in the car and guard the instruments. (A note here:

Bonnie and I shared the same bed because it was cheaper this way. And a lot warmer.)

Slim was back.

"Did your dog like the room?" Snag asked Slim, his thin voice dripping venomous sarcasm with every sneering syllable. Slim didn't answer. He just signed the register and left the motel office, carefully not slamming the screen door.

"Goddamn Mexicans," Snag Hilton said.

"Yeah," Bonnie said. "Too bad there were so many of them at the Alamo—Davy Crockett might be alive today."

"Who's Davy Crockett?" Snag wanted to know.

"Who's Davy Crockett?!" Bonnie said, rather loudly I thought. "That's like asking who's Calvin Coolidge?! Jesus *Christ!*"

"That last one I know," Snag Hilton said, with what he had been using for a smile.

"Good for you, Buster," Bonnie said, at the same time adjusting her C cups to redistribute her out-of-date bosoms. Snag's eyes opened a little wider at this, and he extended his smile to reveal a full set of empty spaces.

Bennie the banjo player, entranced by this, said, "Your teeth are fine but your gums will have to come out."

"What was that?" Snag said.

"It's just a joke," I said. "An old joke. Bennie's a banjo player."

"Has *he* got a dog, too?" Snag wanted to know.

"No," I said. "Slim's the only one with a dog. We almost had a couple of lions, but how many motels would take in lions?"

"That goddamn dog and that goddamn Mexican better behave themselves in that goddamn cottage that's all I gotta goddamn say," Snag goddamn said.

"You're a beautiful person," Bonnie said and left, carefully slamming the screen door so hard both hinges pulled their screws from the doorjamb.

"She broke my door," Snag said.

"Yeah," Bennie said. "Now you'll have every goddamn Mexican mosquito for miles around in here."

Slim appeared, stepping carefully around the prone

screen door, and said, "Big Boy can't sleep—you got an extra pillow? Doesn't have to be new."

"Who's Big Boy?" Snag said, knowing full well.

"He's my dog," Slim said. "He's a Great Dane and he can't sleep without a pillow. There's only one pillow on the bed."

"You got a dog—a Great Dane—sleeping on *my bed?!*" Snag screamed.

"No," Slim said. *"My* bed. I paid four dollars for the night."

Snag turned purplish, then blackish, then whitish, then repeated the process in reverse order.

"Look, you Mexican sonofabitch," he said, his voice strangled by its overconstricted vocal cords.

"Wait a minute," Bennie said. "Why don't you give the Mexican sonofabitch a pillow so we can all get some sleep."

"No," Snag Hilton said. "No! No! No!" By this time, he had lost all control of his saliva. "No! No! No! No!!!!!!!" he frothed. He kept it up for hours. We could still hear him when we were in bed at three o'clock in the morning. By this time it sounded more as if he was conducting an Aztec prayer meeting. It was sort of soothing. And irritating.

The next day, fifty miles beyond Maggie's Nipples, Wyoming, on our way to Yellville, Arkansas, where we had another fabulous one-nighter, Slim told us that we could never stay at the Maggie's Nipples Hilton again.

"Why?" I said. "We *paid* the man."

"Yeah," Slim said, "but Big Boy—well, you know how much he eats—"

"What's that got to do with it?" Bonnie said.

"Plenty," Slim said, "—when his bowels move."

"You don't mean—?" I said.

"Yeah," Slim said. "Right in the middle of the bed. It happened when I was takin' a shower."

"Oh, my God," Bonnie said.

"Yeah," Slim said. "I wrote a little note and stuck it in it. Right at the peak."

"A note?" I said. "What did the note say?"

95

"This happens every time I sleep without a pillow—signed, Fraternally Yours, Big Boy."

Everyone in the Honansville Ecology Group agreed that this was a charming and sad dog story. Alice Dotson wept. And so did Harry Mitchell—but for a different reason.

19

ONE morning after I had returned, exhausted, from walking Wolf through the hills, I received an urgent phone call and ran smack into the Jack Paar dog crisis. Jack always asks my advice on things about which I have not the slightest knowledge—but with the few subjects I *am* an expert in in *all phases,* he has not once, in the years I've known him, sought me out for counsel. Therefore when his dog, Leica, was taken down with some mysterious malady, he called me to ask what I thought it was. Others have made the same mistake, nurturing the misbelief that I had some occult power to diagnose what was wrong with their pets—over the telephone. The truth being, if they would only believe me, I have no knowledge of animal diseases outside of mange (which usually turns out the animal is shedding its winter coat).

Jack Paar's dog had all the symptoms (according to my dog disease book) of distemper, plus dropsy, spasms, paroxysms, apoplexy, locomotor ataxia, beriberi, and a nervous breakdown. The dog, according to Jack on the phone, could not walk without staggering. It had also taken to collapsing in a heap and sleeping where it fell for five or six hours—then awakening, apparently cured of everything. But then the next day the whole process would start over again. The dog, a beautiful German shepherd, would be found when Jack got up in the morning lurching around the living room, knocking over end tables, vases, and delicately innocent floor lamps.

Then it would fall down and sleep. This continued for several days, and Jack finally took the dog to a veterinarian, who could find nothing wrong so he gave the animal a shampoo and a set and sent it home.

On the seventh day *He* rested but Paar didn't. He was too busy with the blind perambulations of Leica, the German shepherd, plus the same sort of behavior from a pet African lion cub who was crashing around the living room, not only knocking everything to the floor but in between staggers tearing the Paars' best couch to shreds. Then it started shredding the drapes, and the rugs, and the Paars. Jack was frantic by this time. He thought his house had been visited by some mysterious and fatal plague. I thought it had, too—then came the great dawning! The great light! There was no fatal plague. There was no deep-seated physical indisposition at all. Not an organic one, anyway. The German shepherd and the lion were drunk! Every night after she finished up after dinner, Mary, the Paars' housekeeper, filled a large pewter dish on the coffee table in front of the fireplace with a pound or so of French brandy-filled chocolates. They were always gone in the morning.

The Paars don't feature brandy-filled chocolates much anymore, but every morning Jack gives the dog and the lion a little shot of Manischewitz. He doesn't want them to think he's a party pooper.

After the Paar dog crisis, we settled down once more to our Honansville way of life. I worked every morning in my top-floor study while Reiko kept busy making rice and vacuuming. Then in the afternoon I played with the animals or chain-sawed some firewood, while Reiko kept busy making rice and vacuuming.

It was a pleasant life—rice was a good, healthy grain to eat and the vacuuming kept out the noise of the TV set and the record player and the radio, which always filled every nook and cranny of our mountaintop house. We had so much noise going we had to add on, at considerable cost, some extra nooks and crannies.

Every day when I went into the pen to play with Wolf, the wolf, and Pussycat, the mountain lion, I felt

97

like I was entering a prison. And I was. It was a prison from which there was no parole. No escape. There they were, these two magnificent animals: Pussycat with her beautiful, nonblinking eyes, purring like a diesel engine and rubbing her lithe, sleek body against my legs; and Wolf, dashing around his pen in the excitement of my visit, wriggling and peeing.

This was their life. Or, I should say, the happiest times of their lives. A few moments' visit from me. A few times a day. The rest of the time was spent either pacing up and down for hours along the steel mesh which held them prisoner or sleeping what I felt was the sleep of despair.

I began to have pangs of remorse about owning them, which on the surface appears ridiculous because, having been born in captivity (a ghastly word), they supposedly knew nothing else. And, to further assuage my rapidly accumulating feeling of guilt, I reasoned, quite correctly, that if *I* didn't have them penned up, someone *else* would. This did very little to diminish my compassion for their plight.

I could never give them all the attention I wanted to—there were so many time-consuming trivialities connected with everyday existence, so many wasteful moments spent trying to telephone someone, or straighten out the stupid and incessant bookkeeping mistakes of computer-burdened companies, and the thousand and one other completely unnecessary petty tasks foisted upon us by the world we all had stupidly helped to create.

I knew the darkness that filled the souls of caged animals. I wanted to make them know I understood. I wanted them to know how much I loved them. To know that they would always be safe and cared for. They would never go hungry or be shot, or trapped, or poisoned. I wanted them to understand all that, but they never would. They'd never understand anything but *freedom*. The one thing I could not give them. But finally, I wanted to—desperately.

20

I HAD long ago contacted the superintendent of the Isle Royale National Park—the only wolf sanctuary in the United States, situated on a remote island in the northwest portion of Lake Superior—asking that if anything happened to me, would he allow my beneficiaries to free in the park any of my wolves who might survive me. The superintendent, Mr. Bruce Miller, was sorry but it would be impossible, he wrote, because the wolf packs or pack now resident in the park—some twenty-five wolves in all—would either kill or wound any wolf strangers. He cited examples of wolves having floated on the ice or crossed the ice from the Canadian mainland, fifteen miles away, during a particularly frigid winter. These wolves—mostly individuals—were immediately, or eventually, attacked by a pack of Isle Royale wolves and maimed so badly that they died or managed, in a few cases, to struggle back across the ice to the mainland.

In the case of Pussycat there was no one to write to. Mountain lions are slaughtered indiscriminately. I know of no refuge for them.

This, then, is why Wolf and Pussycat were still in pens here in Connecticut. If I were wealthy enough, instead of giving money to the *organizers,* who stand between the donor and the recipient of all the millions of dollars given for refugee children, starving aborigines, and shoeless Indians, I would like to endow a wild animal park limited to the less popular of the endangered species such as the wolf, the mountain lion, the alligator, the eagle and the hawk, and the many other so-called predators. An unfortunate term for the *few* when we are *all* indeed "predators." We all kill to eat—that is, the normal person does. The rest kill for pleasure and in desperation to prove that underneath their thermal pantyhose they're really *men!* These woodsy closet queens just *adore* those darling red coats and their jaunty red hunting caps, which works out fine because red is a very good color to wear in the forest—makes it easier for the hunters to "accidentally" blast each other. And who's to blame whom? It's a great legal way to get rid of a business rival or just some guy whose wife you covet (if you have any male hormones left after the "hunt"). ⤳

Before I stop frothing at the mouth here, let me put forth one more choice bit of woodslore: According to the rules of hunting safety, you should never wear a white handkerchief sticking out of your jacket pocket —you might be mistaken for a white-tailed deer. Which gives us another insight on this glorious and "spiritually uplifting" (according to an article reprinted in the Connecticut *Wildlife Conservation Bulletin*) sport. This helpful hint about the white handkerchief indicates that in spite of the covers you see on *Field and Stream* and *Outdoor Life,* and other magazines, of a magnificent white-tailed buck erect and *facing* the hunter, most white-tailed deer are shot in the rectum. Which is *really* spiritually uplifting! Right on! Eh, *Sportsmen?*

My idea of a wildlife park I thought I might be able swing right here in the still relatively unpopulated woods of the Honansville area. I had not the money, and I was not sure that I could raise enough through popular subscription for such unpopular birds and beasts and reptiles. But I thought I would give it a try. Because once these few we have left are gone—*they are gone.*

"We can always produce more children," Harry Mitchell said one night at the monthly meeting of the Honansville Ecology Group, "but what about the passenger pigeon?"

"What about the passenger pigeon?" Ruthie Mitchell, Harry's semilovely wife, wanted to know.

"Well," Harry started, after a long, deep draft of his martini, which I had knowingly served him in a King Henry VIII brandy snifter (it must have held a quart and a half, at least), "the last passenger pigeon died in 1914, in Cincinnati."

"Oh, that's terrible," Ruthie Mitchell said. "Where was it going?"

"It wasn't *going* anywhere," Harry said, with beautiful patience. "It *lived* in Cincinnati."

"Why?" Mr. and Mrs. Rogers Dotson chorused from down deep in their Norfolk jackets, turtlenecked sweaters, and Pepto-Bismoled viscera.

"Why?!" questioned Harry Mitchell, with an indignation that caused abnormal tides in his tankard of martini, which overflowed onto the wetlands of his red suede vest. "Why does *anybody* live in Cincinnati????"

"That's what *I'd* like to know, too," Mr. Dotson said, smoking his polluted meerschaum and stroking the head of the nonexistent faithful old Irish setter.

Harry Mitchell had just about had it from Mr. and Mrs. Rogers Dotson not because of their holier-than-thou attitude and their clenched-teeth accents, but because Harry was in the insurance business and they wouldn't buy a policy from him. This, I felt, was behind Harry's edginess in any conversation with the Dotsons.

"We *liked* Cincinnati," Reiko said. "When Jack and I were doing a nightclub act we played Cincinnati—we liked it."

"That was Kansas City, dear," I said, as gently as I could.

"What's the difference?" Reiko asked. There was nothing I could say to this.

"For Chrisake!" Bella Brown let go with her moose-call bellow. "Let's have another drink and get down to the goddamn reason we're here—Jack, the booze is a little slow tonight."

"Well," I said, pouring triples for everyone, "the reason we are here tonight is to raise some money for a wildlife refuge, or farm, someplace where we can protect and maybe propagate some endangered species."

"Say," Virgil Palmquist said, with a pronounced lisp and a gesture that would never be interpreted as a stand for Black Power (Virgil had *never* clenched his fist except to hold a bouquet of pussywillows), "I *like* that. Maybe Reggie and I could open up a little antique stand branch somewhere in the vicinity and sell a few antiques to all the city folks who come up to see the animals!"

"Oh," Reggie Mailer, Virgil's antique shop partner, said, "how divine! How utterly divine!" Then he kissed Virgil.

"How about me?" Harry Mitchell burped. Then Reggie kissed Harry.

"For Chrisake, Reggie!!! I meant how about me selling a little insurance up there—you know, in case somebody gets bit?"

"Wait a minute," I said. "We're not planning on a shopping center where you can get anything you want."

"What's so wrong with shopping centers?" Alice Dotson, who happened to own several, asked.

"Speaking of whores," Harry Mitchell said, a sudden faraway look in his orange eyes, "did I ever tell everybody about the whore in Butte, Montana, who had this dog and—"

"Anybody like-a more tea?" Reiko asked.

"Harry," I said, "why don't you quit selling insurance and write dog stories?"

"Or whore stories," Virgil Palmquist said. "Everybody *knows* all the *dog* stories—"

"The kid's got an idea," Harry said. " 'A Whore and His Dog—' how does that grab you?"

"How about 'Lad: a Whore'?" asked Reggie Mailer.

"I think 'Lassie: a Whore' would be more appropriate," Harry said.

Bella Brown aimed a half pint of tobacco juice at the large pail we kept by her side for just this purpose and missed, drowning Doggie, our little Pomeranian.

21

THE first week of the Honansville Ecology Group's drive for funds to establish a wildlife refuge for predators started off a little slow. We were competing with the United Fund, which seemed to have a much more universal appeal than the saving of a few endangered wolves, wildcats, and black-footed ferrets. To make people aware, we tried the Madison Avenue scare technique to convince them that their future lives would be as nothing without a few wolves running around in the wilderness. The public didn't buy this at all, and some of them got downright nasty when it came to the black-footed ferret. They said they wouldn't contribute one single penny to a black-footed *anything!*

All this resistance didn't bother us too much. The United Fund wasn't having such smooth going, either. The big red thermometer erected on the village green was below freezing for a long time. People were not in the mood to contribute to the support of babies born out of wedlock anymore. This seemed uncharitable to me, but as Old Man Slawson, the proprietor of Slawson's drugstore, remarked, "Let the bastards who sired the bastards support the bastards. I got all *I* can do to pay my *rent!*" Old Man Slawson's attitude may not be typical. I think he had been disappointed in the sale of the Pill this year, mainly because some of the Honansville brood sows, called Mother by hordes of runny-nosed offspring, didn't believe in the Pill. "It ain't natural," Mrs. Claude Frisbie said. Mrs. Claude Frisbie was eighty-three years old and took five a day. She wasn't afraid of getting pregnant, it was just "that they make me feel young again," she explained. They not only made her "feel young": When she went to the Honansville picture show to see an Omar Sharif movie she had to be chained to her seat. All this according to Old Man Slawson.

There was something else which wasn't exactly a plus in our drive for funds for endangered species:

The Honansville Ecology Group was known locally as the Bleeding Heart and Booze Society. Not without some justification. And we owed it all, or at least the last designation, to our very own Harry Mitchell.

Harry Mitchell, after several buckets of martinis, became the world's greatest driver. Ruthie Mitchell, his semilovely wife, became the world's greatest co-pilot. They were so good that almost every night after our monthly meeting, the Honansville police would stop them on their way home. Especially on snowy winter nights. The Honansville police were curious as to why the parking meters, placed intermittently along the village green, were being used as markers for a downhill slalom run by a little red 1968 Volkswagen. Harry explained, quite logically, that the village green was *downhill,* and *he* was Jean-Claude Killy. After the police, as a formality, had asked to see his driver's license and patiently explained to him that his name was Harry Mitchell, Harry Mitchell reluctantly agreed. Always Harry Mitchell was let off with a warning—mainly, I think, because the police, as everyone in Honansville, liked him. And everybody had always looked up to Harry Mitchell as the town drunk. It wasn't much of an honor, but Harry was invariably pointed out to summer visitors by other summer visitors as a man who lurched to a different drum.

The Honansville police rarely became annoyed or concerned by Harry's drunk driving, but when he started barreling through backyards and over people's lawns and (he told us) leapfrogging (not lengthwise) over the few swimming pools in town, they began to chase him, which was exactly what the looped Harry Mitchell had in mind.

Some nights it took the police quite some time to catch up with Harry. He had so many cute drunk-driving tricks, which he saved until just the right moment. His *best* trick he saved as a surprise—one night while being hotly pursued he drove into an old, extremely narrow Connecticut covered bridge, followed by the cops—then he quickly turned around as he came out of the other end of the covered bridge and drove *right back into* it again. The first and only time he tried this trick his timing was perfect, and he met the wailing police car right smack in the middle. The cops reacted with terrified shrieks as they brought their squad car to a screaming halt. Front bumpers touching.

The Honansville police never chased Harry Mitchell after that. They were so upset over this covered bridge near miss that after it happened no one would volunteer for night duty on the nights the Honansville Ecology Group had its monthly meeting. No cop would leave the safety of the squad room until after Harry Mitchell had his driver's license suspended for driving along the railroad tracks fifteen feet in front of the midnight freight to Pittsfield. A Connecticut state trooper spotted him, and despite Harry's protest that the midnight freight to Pittsfield had been dangerously tailgating him, the trooper saw to it that Harry became an overnight pedestrian.

This dismayed Harry not a bit. He bought an old saddle horse, and on his zonked-out first trip back to his home after a group meeting, as he passed through the village he yelled, "Mick Jagger is coming! One if by land—two if by sea!" This earned him a backside full of rock salt fired by an irate farmer who didn't appreciate Harry or his message or having his sleep interrupted at three in the morning when he had to get up at four.

Harry never knew he had received a full charge of rock salt, because he was too drunk, but from that night on he always wondered why his *derrière* seemed to be spotted like a flabby pink leopard. He thought it was something he had picked up at an unsterile Holiday Inn.

By the time the Honansville Ecology Group's drive was in its third month, we were in third place behind the United Fund and Bonds for Bangladesh and were thinking seriously about giving up the idea of a wildlife refuge for Honansville. We also ran into a little opposition from another organization, made up chiefly of fourteen-year-olds who wanted not only peace, but peace with green stamps. I don't know how sincere they were, but they did paint peace signs all over the old World War II tank which stands in the village green, its one big gun zeroed in on the Bide-a-Wee Funeral Home. (There's a reason for this positioning. It seems that the city fathers decided, when they first brought the tank to Honansville, if the big gun ever did go off accidentally, nobody would get hurt.)

I felt that the Honansville Ecology Group, who deep down, for all their love of fun and alcohol, did have compassion for the wild creatures of this earth, wasn't helping me and my conscience. I knew that somehow, with or without a wildlife refuge, I had to set Wolf free—Pussycat, the mountain lion, never, but Wolf somehow must be given a chance. If it could be done with an African lion, whose intelligence quotient is below the wolf's, why couldn't it be done with a wolf?

I had written to Joy Adamson, the wonderful woman of *Born Free* celebrity, through Mr. Paar, and she advised me that a wolf would present quite a different problem from Elsa, because lions are relatively protected (now), while every hand is raised against the wolf. There is no bounty on lions. No government hunters. No cyanide guns. And no killers sitting in the relative comfort of a small plane or helicopter as used in chasing a wolf in open country until it drops paralyzed with exhaustion and waits hopelessly and helplessly to be murdered. And even then, as a "conservation" officer in Minnesota reported, after exhausting a wolf with a snowmobile, as he approached it on foot to kill it, the wolf wagged its tail in the friendly submissive gesture of a whipped dog. He killed it.

I had thought of this risk, but there *have* been cases of some outstanding wolves who have outwitted man over a period of many years. Old Three Toes, a famous South Dakota wolf, supposedly raided ranches in that area for thirteen years and avoided capture by at least 150 hunters during that time. He was finally killed when he was very old and virtually helpless—or so the brave legend goes in South Dakota. South Dakota is also celebrated for the massacre at Wounded Knee.

My problem in teaching Wolf how to return to a wild which he had never known was that I had to teach him, or at least let him learn, how to hunt. And to do this I needed some sort of something for him to hunt. I couldn't very well start out with an old moose for him to practice on, because, number one, who sold old mooses? Not Korvette's. And secondly, I could never stand by and watch Wolf kill an old moose. Or an old cow. Or an old anything. I knew this sort of thing went on with wild wolves, but it was not my idea of a spectator sport.

On our walks Wolf had always caught field mice, which I understand are rightly called voles. This was and is a very large part of the wild wolf's diet—strange as it may seem to readers of "Little Red Riding Hood" and "The Three Little Pigs."

Pouncing on the unsuspecting, and little-prepared, field mice (as I shall call them) was something a wolf will do even if he is on the end of a twenty-pound chain leash, and this is just what Wolf had been doing every time he walked me through the woods and fields. Whether he ever actually caught a mouse it was difficult to discover, because when I would move toward him to investigate the mouthful of grass or leaves, which might have also contained a mouse, he would growl a warning. It was the only time he growled at me that I had no reason to doubt his sincerity.

In order to ensure a greater supply of field mice, which I still did not have complete evidence of his capturing, I had to take Wolf farther and farther away from the wolf-pen and deeper and deeper into the hardwood forest which covered this part of Connecticut.

Some of the trails we followed were tricky, with many slippery moss-covered rocks to scramble over. And many fallen trees. A man by himself would have had a difficult journey on these woodland paths, but with Wolf tugging and straining to break into a run, the simple woodland path became a deadly obstacle course. I always told Reiko which part of the woods I would be in (we had every area sectionalized, so if one did not return from a walk, the survivors would know where to look for one's body). I felt that someday I might get dragged way off course by this superbeast and trip over something and maybe break a leg. So then what would I do? Nobody would know where to look for me, and I couldn't very well drag a broken leg and a wolf back to home base.

I also had some other very unpleasant thoughts along this line: Suppose I should be rendered unconscious by a falling tree on my head, or some natural disaster like a touch of yellow fever, or a coral-snake bite, or whatever it is that strikes down happy-go-lucky writers? What would happen to Wolf? He was chained to my right wrist. Would he simply lie down beside me and die, too, like a faithful old wolf? Or would he chew off my arm and run away into the forest looking for wolf broads? Either way it was a lousy choice.

Our daily sorties into the hunting field were less than noteworthy. I think Wolf caught a few field mice, and I know for sure he once grabbed a small rabbit, which must have been the stupidest rabbit in all of New England. It apparently just stayed right next to the path and let itself be snatched up by Wolf's enormous jaws. It was a merciful death because it was so quick, or so I liked to think.

After the rabbit incident, I wasn't so sure I wanted to go through with the rest of it. Sooner or later, I knew I would have to take him to Canada, where he'd have to learn on his own how to kill something a little bigger, and smarter. And I would have to be the "Godfather" who would have to make the "arrangements," so Wolf would be able to Puzo an old moose.

22

"I DON'T know how I can do it," I said to Reiko one dreary evening after a TV dinner she had cooked perfectly: The entree was a slice of plastic chicken, with a side order of gray peas that a dwarf could have played fourwall handball with, musk-flavored library paste mashed potatoes, and a round slice of artificially colored, artificially preserved, artificial cranberry jelly, which tasted like an artificial red hockey puck (try it—you'll like it).

The weather was mostly outside, except in one corner of our living room where it dropped soft rains into endlessly changed buckets and pots. I had been determined, early in life, never to allow the weather, no matter how depressing, to control my naturally sunny disposition; but I have never conquered my avidity to hang myself in the bathroom at the slightest drop in the barometer. Something happens to my psyche when Gary Essex tells me the humidity is 100 percent on the CBS six-o'clock news, and a few minutes later Dr. Frank Field on the NBC six-o'clock news and Tex on the ABC six-o'clock news tell me the same thing. I never heard any of them ever explain *how* the humidity could be 100 percent, unless you were living at the bottom of a lagoon.

"You don't know how you can do *what?*" Reiko asked.

"I don't know how I can send Wolf out into the forest all by himself," I said. This was after a particularly bad day Wolf and I had spent combing the hills for miles around, it seemed, for mice or stupid rabbits. Either there were no mice or stupid rabbits left, or Wolf preferred something a little less bland. His interest in the hunt had also waned considerably. He wanted more to run crazily in circles—at the end of his heavy chain—which was all right in open ground, but not in the woods where, if I didn't jump over the circling steel chain quickly enough, I'd find myself lashed to a tree, staked —like the last scene in *Joan of Arc*. I hated to admit it, but I felt that Wolf would never be able to fend for himself. He would starve to death, running in crazy circles, having fun.

"I have an idea," Reiko said. "I've just thought of something."

"You just thought of a brand-new place you can vacuum!"

"No," Reiko said sincerely. "I've vacuumed everything that I can reach with that cord. It's only a fifty-foot cord, you know."

"How about vacuuming the Housatonic River?" I said. "Looks pretty dusty."

Reiko laughed at this and said I was silly and would I get her a longer cord the next time we went down to Honansville. I had a feeling the Housatonic was going to look a lot tidier very soon.

"Don't you want to hear my idea?" Reiko said.

"What's the idea?" I said.

"Yeah, Mommie," Bobby said. "What's the big idea?"

"Big idea," Timothy said.

"Why don't you get a female wolf?"

This almost flattened me, knowing that Reiko wasn't too fond of the wolf we had—now she was proposing I ger *another* animal she could dislike.

"You're kidding!" I said. "Have you been talking to Dr. Shimkin?"

"No," Reiko said. "I think Wolf needs to have a wife. It's *my* idea."

"A wolf wife," Bobby said.

"Wife," Timothy said, playing his part of Little Sir Echo all the way.

"Jesus Christ!" I said. "I could never figure out the female of the species in the white race; now I've got to puzzle over the Japanese version!"

"What's that mean?" Reiko said.

"I just don't understand—that's what it means. You don't like Wolf and now you're suggesting we get a mate for him! You want wolf puppies all over the place?"

"I love wolf puppies," Bobby said. "I really *love* wolf puppies!"

"Love—woof—puppy," Timothy said. Which was almost his first sentence.

"I don't mean for them to have puppies here," Reiko said. "I mean—out in the woods."

"Oh."

"You said that one wolf wouldn't last long in the woods by himself. How about two wolves?"

This was a very valid question and something that John and Sandra Harris, the founders of the North American Association for the Preservation of Predatory Animals, were doing out in the West.

John and Sandra were placing a whole family of domesticated wolves in carefully selected wilderness reserves, a male, his mate, and four, five, or six puppies—whatever the litter consisted. This way, *theoretically,* the wolf family would be conscious of the need for providing for itself. Or, I should say, the need would be more poignantly stressed than if a wolf were all alone in an alien environment. The Harrises reasoned that the fact of a kindred group, with many mouths to feed, would inspire the male—who does most of the hunting while the female stays with the pups—to arouse all the instincts of his latent wildness and quickly learn the technique required to feed a voracious family. Although hunting for the first time and alone, the male could hardly be expected to bring down anything large, he could with luck and a lot of legwork bring home enough to sustain his mate and her pups. A single wolf *can* kill a deer by the ambush method, which a wolf uses because he could not hope to *outrun* one. A wolf will wait above a deer trail, crouching on a ledge; and when an unsuspecting deer gets within range, the wolf streaks down from its hiding place with such a rush that the deer has no time to even think about running and is killed.

Most deer, especially if they are old or in poor condition from starvation, take to the frozen lakes and rivers when they are in danger of a wolf attack. This is a mistake for them, because a wolf can usually drive them into the cul-de-sac of some small bay or cove, with steep banks surrounding it. Thus a cornered animal can usually be brought down with little difficulty by a strong wolf.

I knew that Wolf, if and when he could be released into the Ontario wilderness, could not have any of the strategy and prowess of a wolf born in the wild; but after he had had enough of mice, rabbits, and other small game, I felt sure he would soon tackle larger prey. He'd have to—the appetite of his family would demand it.

If this account of how a wolf survives in the wild seems too casual and callous in the telling and conjures

up the horrifying picture of Bambi being slaughtered—
that is exactly what happens. Just as it happens to other
creatures every hour of the day and night at Swift &
Co.

23

"I DON'T know," I said. "Maybe it
wouldn't work." What I meant was maybe some sonofabitch might shoot Wolf on his first day on his own.
They're still fair (?) game in Canada, and if the wolves
of Canada are wiped out, that's *all* there is—except
Alaska. And the way Alaskans are going, there won't be
any up there either. With all the "progress" the Alaskans
are pushing for, there won't be much of *anything* left—
except a long, leaky pipeline and a few old Indians selling Made-in-Hong-Kong toy totem poles and one polar
bear rug.

"If you want to free our wolf," Reiko said, "the least
you can do is give him a family. It's nice to have a
family."

"Oh, *really?*"

"Yes—a family means happiness."

"Maybe you're right," I said, remembering Ma Barker.

"Do you know anybody who's got a female wolf?"
Bobby asked.

"Yeah," Timothy said, "fe-male woof."

"That's 'wolf,' " I said.

"Woof," Timothy said.

"Maybe he's right," I said. Then I started mumbling
to myself—a habit which I am developing into a full-
time career. There's *so much* to mumble about.

"Where can I find an adult female woof?"

"Wolf," Timothy said.

"Maybe Old Lady Simpson," Reiko said, although I
don't know how she remembered the name.

"Yeah," I said. "Maybe I'll drive up and see her tomorrow."

"Why don't you just call her?" Reiko said. I couldn't tell Reiko that I didn't want to *call* her—I wanted to *see* her. A man doesn't see too many Old Lady Simpsons in his time. I wanted to gaze once more on the mountains of the moon and the valley of the Nile. And the hanging gardens of Babylon.

"What do you mean—*call* her?" I said, too defensively. "I'm not going to buy a wife for Wolf over the phone! I gotta look her over. See if she's suitable."

"Gee," Bobby said. "That's funny!"

"It is?" I said. "What is?"

"It's gonna be Wolf's wife, but *you* gotta check her out."

"Right," I said. "And when *you* get old enough to choose a wife, I'm gonna check *her* out, too."

"Why?" Bobby said. "I'm not gonna marry a female wolf."

"That's why I'm gonna check her out," I said. "You can't be too careful these days."

"Papa," Bobby said, "you're a nut!"

"Bobby!" Reiko said, as she was getting the vacuum cleaner ready for another voyage through dustland. "That's no way to talk about your crazy father!"

This whole scene was developing into something from O'Neill's *Long Day's Journey into Night,* where everybody in the family, including the dog and the goldfish, is a junkie, so I tried to switch the subject, which was very hard to do over the varooming of the Ferrari vacuum cleaner Reiko was now cornering in the living room.

Old Lady Simpson's spermy voice on the phone made me feel like I used to feel like when I lived the life of a bachelor in Hollywood at a place called the Garden of Allah. The Garden of Allah is gone now, and so was I, until I talked to Old Lady Simpson. But it was to no avail. Old Lady Simpson had no female wolves old enough for Wolf. She explained in that cello voice of hers that a female had to be at least twenty-two months

113

old before it can be bred. And in this climate it usually happens around the first of February.

"Just once a year?" I said.

"Yes," Old Lady Simpson said. "That's sufficient for wolves—and most animals."

"Oh," I said. "Sounds like a pretty dull life." There was no reply to this and I immediately felt like the leading man in act one of an obscene phone call. I wanted to ask her if she was wearing those wild hot pants. This always seems to be one of the first questions asked by obscene phone callers: "What are you wearing?" The heavy breather wants the recipient of his call to reply, *"Nothing!* I'm standing here in this cold, drafty hallway *absolutely naked* answering your phone call!" But, according to a poll taken recently by *The Village Voice,* most women who are fortunate enough to receive these calls are standing in a cold drafty hallway wearing leather pants and a plaid Mackinaw and carrying a shopping bag from Bloomingdale's filled with goodies shoplifted from Klein's. This doesn't make the obscene phone caller feel any closer to fulfillment or the Nixon administration. And Bloomingdale's shopping bags tend to turn him off. They're sexually symbolic but much too impersonal.

I'm sure all of this sounds weird to the reader. And it is. If I had more free time I'd work at being oversexed. Or Kurt Vonnegut.

24

THE first of February. The wolf-breeding season for our latitude was growing close, and I was becoming more and more frustrated with each passing day. I simply could not find a mate for Wolf. I called the few animal dealers I knew of, most of whom were at least a three-dollar phone call from us, and none had

114

a female timber wolf suitable for my purposes. Maybe a better way to say it would be for *Wolf's* purposes.

One game farm slicker tried to get me to take a female fox, advising *me,* confidentially, that no one would know the difference. No one but the prospective bridegroom, I advised *him.*

Wolf was growing more and more restive as the pangs of his budding maturity gave him ideas. He no longer wanted me as a pal—or so it seemed. I had been both mother and father and big brother to him, but like all males—if they have enough hormones—this is not enough when you reach your high-octane puberty level. Wolf was ready, I felt, for anything. Even a fox. Or a careful porcupine.

Finally, Sandra Harris came to the rescue. She found a lovely two-year-old female who had been raised on the roof of a small apartment house in San Francisco.

"What's the matter with it?" I asked Sandra on the phone. "Why do the people want to get rid of it?"

"Well," Sandra said, "all the while they've had it up on the roof of their apartment, nobody knew it was there and no one complained. But a couple of months ago they built a high-rise right next door and the new neighbors looked out from the tiny balconies of their expensive little apartments and found they were face to face with a wolf—and they all started to raise hell."

"Why?" I said. "Did the wolf reach out and eat the geraniums out of their flower boxes or something?"

"She didn't do anything." Sandra said. "The people in the new high-rise just don't want to look out from their balconies and see a wolf."

"What *do* they want to see?" I asked.

"Alcatraz," Sandra said. "That's the way they advertised this new apartment: 'Sit on your very own balcony and on a clear day you can see forever and Alcatraz.' "

"What a beautiful inducement," I said.

"Yes," Sandra said, "and from the higher-priced apartments you can see forever and San Quentin."

"Beautiful," I said. "Beautiful and *different.*"

115

"Yes," Sandra said. "When Tony Bennett comes back to pick up his heart he's gonna see a big change."

That's how we got Lady. "Lady" was the name her former owners had given her, and I saw no reason to change it because that's what we probably would have called her, too, because that's what she was.

She arrived late one Friday night at JFK Airport in a large kennel cage marked in tall yellow letters GERMAN SHEPHERD. This was to thwart any red tape that might suddenly entangle us for having brought a wolf into New York State. I knew it was against the law to bring in a pistol because you might injure some innocent mugger, but I wasn't too sure of the New York statutes on wolves.

On the long drive back to Honansville, which took almost as much time as the flight from California, Reiko said, "This is just like Japan."

"What is?"

"We picked out a wife for Wolf and a husband for Lady without even asking either one of them. Just like Japan."

"You mean they have wolves in Japan?" Bobby immediately wanted to know.

"No," Reiko said and didn't explain further.

"What Mamma means," I said, "is that in Japan the parents choose the girl that their son is going to marry, and he's gotta marry her."

"Oh," Bobby said. Then after daintily prospecting his nose a bit, he continued, "You mean *your* mother and father picked out *Mamma* for you to marry?"

"Yes," I said. "They stuck a pin in the Tokyo phone book, and it went right through Reiko Hashimoto's name."

"Who's Reiko Hashimoto?"

"Your mother."

Bobby didn't believe this. I didn't blame him. And if you stuck a pin in the Tokyo phone book you'd get Sessue Hayakawa. He's on *every* page (start at the right and read *down*.)

Whatever the circumstances of Lady's premarital arrangements, everything worked out fine when I put her

116

into the pen with Wolf. It was love at first sight for both. Wolf started dancing delightedly around Lady, getting down on his knees and wagging his tail like a big friendly dog. Lady responded by placing her forepaws across Wolf's massive shoulders. Then she laid her head across his shoulders and rubbed back and forth, all the while whimpering, almost songlike. This drove Wolf into a Lupercalian ecstasy, and he started dashing around the pen like he had suddenly lost all of his marbles. He was absolutely demented. Lady was also finding it hard to control her sensuous movements—not that there was any reason she had to. She stood with her tail high, moving her rear in an unmistakable gesture of voluptuous invitation. The whole thing was a tableau dedicated to Aphrodite and the Temple of Love. If only Eric Segal had been there.

I'll pull the shade down on the actual mating. Descriptions of this sort of thing don't belong in a family book. Accounts of actual matings don't belong in *any* book—unless you want to make money.

Lady, whose lovely fur was black as a moonless night, was a fine-boned, delicately proportioned Montana timber wolf—that is, her forebears had come from the land of the Big Sky. And although she was very timorous with me at first, after three weeks or so she would approach close enough to allow me to scratch the area just above her full, thick tail, an area wolves seem to like to be scratched. But all the while I rubbed her back, she was ready to spring away if I made any sudden movements.

Wolf did not seem to resent my attentions to his bride. I thought there might be some jealousy, as with dogs, but he never showed any signs of anything but pride. He seemed very proud that he now had a mate, and somehow he was quieter, too, and somewhat more dignified. He didn't jump all over me as he once did at the slightest opportunity. I was happy about this, because a 150-pound wolf suddenly rearing up and placing his enormous paws on my shoulders when I had my back turned did something to my equilibrium. It knocked me flat is what it did. And several times broke my sunglasses. Or if the glasses didn't break they would fly off my nose and Wolf would grab them and nothing could induce him to give them back. He lips would roll back from his huge canine teeth, making him look for all the world like the dire wolf who used to scare the hell out of everybody around the La Brea tar pits about 15,000,000 years ago. I played it smart. Wolf could have all the sunglasses he could eat.

25

"SPEAKING of Butte, Montana—" Harry Mitchell started, "did I ever tell you kind folks and gentle people about—"

"For Chrisake, Harry!" Bella Brown said. "You told us about it eight thousand times!" Then Bella aimed a stream of tobacco juice at the fireplace and she didn't miss. Smokey the Bear wouldn't have to sit up all night worrying. The fire was doused into extinction.

"Bella," I said, "we *needed* that fire. It's cold in here. And why don't you chew something a little less saliva-fomenting? So we all don't have to sit around wondering who's going to need artificial respiration next."

"What's the matter with you?" Bella said, shifting her plug from one side of her mouth to the other. "Don't you like Tiparillos?"

"Only when they're smoked."

"Jesus Christ," Bella said, "a bloody purist!"

"Speaking of purists," Harry Mitchell said, inadvertently slopping his martini into his inadvertently opened fly (Harry was a careless dresser), "did I ever tell you about this college girl in Butte, Montana?"

"College girl?" I said. "What happened to the whore?"

"Same girl," Harry said. "She was working her way through Radcliffe."

"Look," Virgil Palmquist said, stomping his tasseled foot, "this is supposed to be a meeting of the Honansville Ecology Group and not the Honansville Nostalgia Society! I'm goddamn sick and tired of hearing Mr. Mitchell here tell of his *one* experience with the opposite sex!"

"Speaking of the opposite sex," Harry Mitchell said, like a tape recorder set for "repeat," "did I ever tell you about this faggot in Vladivostok? It seems that he didn't make his quota and Stalin had him shot—"

"Gee, Harry," Harry's semilovely wife, Ruthie, said, leaning over and giving Harry a smarmy kisss and at the same time spilling some of *her* martini into Harry's inadvertently open fly, "that sounds interesting!"

"Not to us," Mrs. Rogers Dotson said, indicating her perpetual husband and herself. "And, Mr. Mitchell, your fly is open."

"It's always open," Ruthie Mitchell said. "Harry's like a little boy."

"Then we have nothing to worry about," Virgil Palmquist said to his antique shop partner, Reggie Mailer, who had been sitting primly trying to look like Ginger Rogers or Bette Davis.

"I'll never worry about anything so long as I have you," Reggie said, reaching out his boneless hand and stroking Virgil's Prince Valiant hairdo.

"I think that's sweet," Ethel Krasselt, the Honansville Indian pot maker, said. Then turning to her painter husband. Frank, "Why don't you act like that, Frank?"

"I'll never worry about anything so long as I have you," Frank said and stroked the other side of Virgil's Prince Valiant hairdo. Reggie slapped Frank's paint-spattered hand. Hard.

"I thought we were here tonight," Alice Dotson said, staring down the miles of her carefully cultivated patrician nose at our motley crew, "to see Mr. Douglas' new wolf."

"New pregnant wolf," I said. "She's due to have pups any moment now."

"Just think," Alice Dotson said, "wolves born right here in Honansville—just like before the white men came—"

"Yes," I said.

"*And* the *blacks,*" Alice Dotson added.

"Gets you right where you live, don't it, *Baybee?*"

119

Harry Mitchell said, slapping one of Alice Dotson's lardaceous buttocks, which overbrimmed the tiny antique milking stool she had chosen to sit on. When Alice Dotson had chosen this site of repose, I had hoped that the tiny antique milking stool would remain grounded when she stood up. We didn't want to lose it.

Alice Dotson gasped at Harry Mitchell's boorish gesture. He had never acted this gauche before.

"You do that again," Rogers Dotson said to Harry Mitchell, "and you'll have *Mrs.* Dotson to deal with!" Then he settled back and contentedly drained his gin and tonic and smoked what smelled like whale blubber and dried rabbit dung in his fine old polluted meerschaum.

"I can't wait to see the wolf pups," Reggie Mailer said. "They must be adorable!"

"They're not really," I said, hating to be the one with the disillusionist attitude. "Wolf pups are just grayish little lumps."

"I don't see why we're *always* talking about *wolves* and what we can do for *them!*" Alice Dotson said. "What about the electric eel?! Do you realize that while we're all sitting up here cozy and snug in our comfy Connecticut estates thousands of electric eels are being slaughtered by the fishermen of Bolivia!"

"Wait a minute," I said. "I thought somebody else had electric eels."

"*We* did," Ruthie Mitchell said, "but we switched with the Dotsons. Now Harry and I have moles. You know, those little things under the ground."

"I think we can surmise, correctly, that most of us know what a mole is," I said.

"Good," Ruthie Mitchell said.

"What about the red-winged blackbird?" Ethel Krasselt wanted to know. "That inhuman beast Ernie Saloks, the gravel pit operator, is positively destroying every swamp he can find by dumping all the dirt he doesn't want into them. How long will this go on? There won't be a cattail left! They'll disappear forever."

"What's a cattail?" Rogers Dotson asked.

"That's what the red-winged blackbird sits on!" Ethel Krasselt said, with some impatience.

"Oh, yes," Rogers Dotson admitted. "I think I knew that. 'Cattail'—I must remember that word—*what* sits on it?"

"Look," Bella Brown said, "I'm not the least concerned with the red-winged blackbird and I don't think any of us should be. The *gnu* is one of our most endangered species."

"Who?" asked Harry Mitchell.

"The gnu! That's who!" Bella Brown said, subconsciously flexing her bulging biceps and jutting her prow of a jaw forward. I thought she was going to grab Harry Mitchell and airplane spin him around her head, then fling him into a corner like a sack of grain, but she checked herself just in time.

"I think we have more pressing ecology problems than the gnu," Ruthie Mitchell said, "and Harry agrees with me. Have you seen any moles lately?"

"You mean at parties around town?" Virgil Palmquist wanted to know, in his sniggeringly superior, extremely irritating tone. Reggie, his antique shop partner, joined him with an early-American giggle.

"Moles are very important," Ruthie continued through the gay mists of scorn from the two velvet-suited elves. "They aerate the soil."

"What does that mean?" Alice Dotson wanted to know. Rogers Dotson seemed interested, too.

"It simply means," Ruthie Mitchell, not quite sure but positively, said, "the earth needs to be aerated—badly!"

"I thought," I said to Bella Brown, "that you were interested in saving the wild horses of the West. You were all heated up about them the last time I saw you at Old Man Slawson's drugstore—you were buying Preparation H and false eyelashes."

"I'm still interested in saving the wild horses of the West from the dog food bastards, but why can't I be interested in the gnu? Somebody else got the gnu?" She looked around the room. Nobody else had the gnu but they all had drinks. I thought sadly to myself, maybe this would be all the Honansville Ecology Group would ever be—a society for well-meaning lushes. Although Harry Mitchell was the only one I would classify as that, at the moment. I felt the others would soon be joining him on that lofty plane.

"You know the gnu?" Bella asked.

"Yes, Bella," I said. "I know the gnu and let's not fool around with that kind of phraseology. The next thing you know we'll be doing a routine." I tried to sound like Groucho Marx, as I said, "Do you know the gnu? No, but I knew the gno."

Bella had never heard of Groucho, so I was wasting my time. She took another great gulp of her beer and bourbon, bit off a large chunk from her well-gnawed slab of Mail Pouch, and said, "The gnu is also known as the wildebeest."

"Yeah," Harry Mitchell said, "also known as Huntington Hartford the Third. Right, Bella?" Before Bella, whose temper lacked the slightest control, could belt Harry Mitchell with what I would bet would be a low blow, she was diverted by Ethel Krasselt.

"What about the skinks?" Ethel Krasselt said. "The earth also needs skinks," she said, elbowing her husband. "Doesn't it, Frank?"

"Jesus H. Kool-Aid!" Harry Mitchell said too loudly, while wringing out his fly. "What the *hell* is a *skink?*"

"A skink," Reggie Mailer said solemnly, "is a cross between a skunk and a mink." Then he and Virgil burst into a fit of uncontrollable laughter. They were convulsed. So much so they both finally started to cry.

Ethel Krasselt waited for this unseemly interruption to subside, then said to Reggie, "Oh, go shove your hanky up your sleeve'!'

"What *is* a skink?" I asked Ethel, slipping into my unhappy role of the perfect host.

"Well," Ethel said, "they're very rare."

"I'll bet," Bella Brown said.

"A skink." Ethel said, ignoring Bella, the Philistine, "is a tropical lizard having a thick, shiny body and short, fat legs."

"That's *her*," Harry Mitchell said. "That whore in Butte, Montana! She was gorgeous!"

"Anybody like-a tea?" Reiko said. She didn't understand the conversation, but her Japanese instinct told her that a little tea couldn't hurt. No one wanted tea, and I marveled at the way Ruthie Mitchell went along with everything Harry said. I wondered if this was the way they acted at home when they were alone. I wondered how any woman would react to a husband who was continually bragging about a two-dollar conquest in Butte, Montana. But before I could do much mental meandering, Rogers Dotson said, "I thought we came over here tonight to see Jack's new wolf."

"Maybe we misunderstood, Father," Alice Dotson said (she always called her husband Father, although they were childless; or maybe they had children they didn't care to mention now that the voting age has been lowered).

"Let's go home, Mother," Rogers Dotson suggested to his wife.

"No," I said. "Wait. I want you all to see Lady."

"Who's Lady?" Virgil Palmquist said.

"It's our new wolf—a mate for Wolf—our old wolf. It's a female," I said.

"I might have guessed *that!*" Virgil said snappishly.

"Come on, everybody," I said, "to the wolf pen!"

The visit to the wolf pen proved to be somewhat of a disappointment. It was dark, and although I had the floodlights turned on, Lady managed somehow to stay in the shadows and act very spooky, and Wolf was less than friendly at such a large group of boisterous and unruly strangers. Always, no matter where we moved around the pen, Wolf placed his body between us and Lady. I really didn't know for sure, but I felt that Lady was going to have her pups very soon, or else Wolf would not have been so protective. Wary, yes, but not protective. Something was going to happen momentarily, so I herded the Honansville Ecology Group back to the house as quickly as they would allow. Herding blind orangutans would have been easier, but after a time I had them all right were I wanted them—in the house, near the bar.

26

WOLF became a proud father sometime during the night, after the Honansville Ecology Group had been sped on their merry way, Harry Mitchell and his semilovely wife, Ruthie, being the last to leave. Harry drove. I didn't know whether he had regained his driver's license, but a thought crossed my mind as I allowed Harry to get behind the wheel of his car: It was like allowing a retarded elf to take over as captain of a leaky lily pad in the middle of Lake Erie during a hurricane. I made the sign of the cross for the All-state Insurance Company as he careened his station wagon out the driveway—not quite missing our huge iron gateposts.

Lady had five pups, I was able to learn after risking the protective wrath of Wolf by poking my head into the wooden wolf den (wolves usually dig their dens into the side of a sandy hill or use the enlarged dens of other animals, but this was not possible in the captive state). Wolf growled and acted very vicious, but I took John Harris' word that he would never bite—and he didn't, although I'm sure the thought crossed his mind.

Lady did not seem concerned at all. She also wagged her tail just a little. She was somewhat dragged out after her ordeal and wanted to lie there and rest. After I counted the pups and made sure they were all alive and presumably well—I had no way of knowing other-wise—I left her. Outside, as I started to open the gate and leave the pen, Wolf came up and stood next to me, acting for all the world like he wanted me to under-stand his behavior of a few moments before. He was just being a father. A wolf father. I understood.

On the fourteenth day after Lady had her pups their eyes were open, but they still seemed to be more or less on the blind side. They stayed in their wooden den close to their mother, but they were walking fairly well, and growling at each other, and chewing at the few bits of salt hay that Lady had left in the den. I had prepared a nice warm nest for her to have her babies, but this did not meet with her approval at all; and long before she gave birth, she scratched most of it outside. This was as it was in the wild. Wolf dens are notorious for their austerity and discomfort.

I couldn't tell how many of the five furry little things were males and how many females, and, again, they didn't look like wolves at all. Their ears were just tiny gray flaps, and their noses were very short and pushed in. Their whole appearance was such that, even though I *knew* better, I could not visualize them growing up to look like wolves. They looked like baby pug dogs. I called Sandra Harris for reassurance. She laughed.

"Don't worry," Sandra said. "In six months they'll look just like Disney wolves. Their noses will be long and pointy and they will be the most wolfishy-looking wolves you ever saw."

"I hope so," I said. "From the looks of them now it looks like Lady had been messing around with a hairy Polish midget. With *no* nose. Just *nostrils.*"

"That could never happen," Sandra said. "Hairy Polish midgets never mate with wolves."

"Sandra," I said, "where did you acquire this vast knowledge of hairy Polish midgets?"

"Well," Sandra said, "I think it was in *TV Guide* —or *The Kiplinger Letter*—or maybe it was something Rex Reed said about some movie with Dennis Hopper."

"Rex Reed said Dennis Hopper was a hairy Polish midget?"

"Well, maybe not in so many words—"

"Sandra," I said, "thank you for your vote of confidence about the wolf pups. I'll send you a picture when I get one."

"Don't forget to autograph it."

As soon as I hung up I wondered if Sandra thought I was going to send her a picture of *me*. This always happens—as soon as I terminate a long-distance call, I

125

have loose ends. I can never learn to ask people that final question which would make everything clear. As a consequence of this I have at least 25,000 unanswered questions cluttering my skull. Questions that will never be answered in my lifetime. Or any lifetime. And I can't discard this accumulation, because I never throw anything away. A writer is like people who subscribe to *National Geographic*—they never throw them away. I have never known anyone, or anyone who has *known* anyone, who has purposely thrown away a single issue of *National Geographic*—because some long winter's evening they are going to reread them. This can be a voluminous hobby, this collecting of *National Geographics*. Where to store them can be an awesome question. Houses overflow with copies. Large barns overflow. I read of one man whose tremendous collection endangered the living space around him. This was when the government of Lichenstein asked him to move to a larger country. And Rhode Island had just passed a law against hoarders of anything larger than pamphlets.

Despite Sandra Harris' confidence, the wolf pups still didn't look like the pups of a wolf—even at the age of three weeks. It was then that they started to venture forth from their wooden den box. They romped with each other, biting and growling and trying their best to act like wolves, but their appearance was against them. They looked like a five-pack of Sears' floor polishers.

I discovered, with some difficulty because of Wolf's resumed belligerency and protectiveness, that we had three males and two females. It was easy to tell the females from a distance because they were the trouble-makers. They were the ones who initiated the fights. And there were fights aplenty. Although the males were stronger and larger, and inflicted more damage on the female than the female was capable of inflicting on the male, never once did a female refrain from daily inciting a pier six brawl in which she would wind up yelping back to the protection of Lady, who didn't seem to anxious to coddle any of her brood. I guess this is one way in which the creatures of the wild teach their young

126

that the world isn't all beer and skittles. It's mostly skittles. Played with loaded skittles.

Harry Mitchell and his semilovely wife, Ruthie, were invited over one morning to see the new wolf pups. *Early* one morning. I wanted to catch Harry without a martini in his hand, and I did, but his back pocket bulged suspiciously, making him look like a Green Bay Packer fan on the coldest day they ever had in Green Bay (which is *any* day after August 21st). I knew Harry was ready for any emergency—such as running out of martinis—but he was reasonably rational when he and Ruthie swung into our driveway, just scraping what was left of his right front fender on our iron gatepost.

"Oh, aren't they adorable!" Ruthie said, adjusting her granny glasses to fit her personality.

"That's Bobby and Timothy," I said. "The wolf pups are over here."

Ruthie giggled. "I thought they were kinda big for puppies," she said. Then she spotted the pups and shrieked with pleased surprise, I guess it was. Ruthie seemed to shriek at a lot of things—mostly at Harry and his droll stories. There *are* wives like this, I've discovered. Everything their husbands say is a gem. Harry and his droll stories, which actually was *one* droll story repeated endlessly at cocktail gatherings, always sent Ruthie into paroxysms of uncontrollable mirth. To Ruthie, Harry was Buster Keaton all rolled into one.

Wolf, of course, resented the intrusion of these loud humans; but instead of ducking back and avoiding anything resembling close contact, he stood his ground in front of Lady and the puppies. I could see that this was a bold and almost unendurable role for him because it was against all of his wolf instincts, which was to get the hell away, as fast as he could, from any human. This they had learned in their thousands of years of unfortunate contact with man.

Harry just looked at the six-week-old pups without comment. Harry was a deep thinker, according to Ruthie. Personally, I don't go along with this philosophy at all. I believe that Harry is as far away from being a sage as Timothy Leary is from the Olympic pole vaulting team (although he gets up there very well without the pole). I think Harry Mitchell is what used to be an apt phrase in television—an empty suit. A lampshade. Not that it mattered—I was happy to show the wolf pups to anyone. Later Virgil Palmquist and Reggie Mailer dropped by after a hard day at their antique shop, where, Reggie confided, they had sold almost their entire supply of ancient Indian pots which Ethel Krasselt had just baked the day before.

"Isn't that illegal, selling fake Indian pots?" I asked.

"Not at all," Virgil said. "We have a special dispensation from Jane Fonda."

"What's Jane Fonda got to do with fake Indian pots?" I said.

"Nothing really," Reggie said, "but she's going around the country trying to stir 'em up enough to force the government to give them back the buffalo and Manhattan Island."

"That's ridiculous," I said. "What the hell would the Indians do with Manhattan Island *now?*"

"Sell it to Puerto Rico," Virgil said.

"Oh," I said, not quite knowing what the hell else to say to these two birds-of-paradise who lived in Honansville, Connecticut.

Reggie and Virgil, and also Bella Brown and Frank and Ethel Krasselt, loved the wolf puppies. Frank, who held one, got his index finger pierced in several places by the puppy's extremely sharp teeth, smiled through his blood, and vowed that it wouldn't make any difference.

Rogers and Alice Dotson were not so sure they approved at all. They were concerned with overpopulation. When I explained that wolves were underpopulated —that's why I was raising the pups—Alice said, "Then I suppose it will start all over again in New England."

"What does *that* mean?" I asked.

"When the Pilgrims landed at Plymouth Rock, the Indians were friendly but the wolves weren't—they ate a lot of Pilgrim children."

"You mean like Little Red Riding Hood?" Bobby asked.

"Was she a Pilgrim?" Rogers Dotson wanted to know.

128

"I don't remember reading anything about her in the Mayflower log book."

"Little Red Riding Hood wasn't a Pilgrim; she was Jewish," I said. "So she wasn't eaten by the wolves."

"Why not?" Alice Dotson asked, looking at me through an overdone lorgnette.

"Well," I said, "she was Jewish, but she wasn't kosher."

"And the wolves—?" Rogers Dotson said.

"They were orthodox," I said. I had no way of knowing whether the Dotsons knew we were playing a game, because their faces were carved out of knotty pine and immobile. If they ever smiled, knots would pop out in all directions and they'd have to have face jobs with plastic wood. I don't know and would *never* know *what* amused them—unless they were terribly entertained by *everything* and couldn't show it because they had given their blood —*all* of it—to a needy hemophiliac family.

I'm sure the Dotsons didn't know what I was talking about as I explained the wolf-Pilgrim-Little Red Riding Hood situation. To them Jewish was Jewish—orthodox or reformed. So far as the Dotsons were concerned, they were all the same and they all came from the same place—New York.

Once I asked, "What about Israel?" and Alice Dotson replied, "Their bonds are very good and they never miss a dividend, and if the Indians are still claiming the land, it's just too bad. Everything happened too long ago— they'll just have to stay on their reservations."

When I saw I was getting nowhere with Israel or the Indians, I asked her, "What about the Arabs?" and she informed me she didn't believe that Mr. Dotson and she had any Arab bonds, but to make sure they would re-examine their portfolio. I gave up.

As the pups grew, they were adding about two and a half pounds per week for the females and three and a half pounds a week for the males—which was really pouring it on. We had lots of visitors, a few of whom joined the North American Association for the Preservation of Predatory Animals, of which I am the national chairman —a position of which I have been long in doubt as to what my duties are; but it's nice to be a national chairman of something which isn't a fatal disease.

The wolf pups at the age of four months were maturing rapidly, and the time, I felt, was drawing near for the great experiment. In another couple of weeks I intended to take Wolf, Lady, and the pups up to our Canadian forest home for their final preparation—such as it was—for release into the thousands of miles of wilderness which surrounded our remote lodge. They would be free and, I guess, in a way so would I.

27

"SAY, aren't you Jack Douglas and his lovely wife, Reiko?" the Canadian customs man asked, as we were stopped on the Canada side of the Niagara River.

"Yes," I admitted carelessly.

"I've seen you on *The Jack Paar Show*, the Johnny Carson show, *The Merv Griffin Show*, *The Dick Cavett Show*, *The Mike Douglas Show*, and with Virginia Graham, and that's how they always introduce you—Jack Douglas and his lovely wife, Reiko."

"We've also been on *He Said—She Said* with Joe Garagiola," Reiko said.

"Oh, yeah," the customs man said. "The funny wop. I like him—he's *really* funny."

"The funny *Italian*," I corrected.

"Yeah," the customs man agreed. "The funny Italian wop. You folks gonna stay in Canada long?"

"Yes," I said.

"What is the purpose of your visit?" the customs man said—sing-song.

"We live here," I said.

"Oh," he said, looking at our Connecticut license plates. "Driving a stolen car, huh?"

"Yes," I said. "Had to steal it last week—takes us quite a while to load up."

"What kinda animals you got in those cages?" he asked, chuckling at my devastating wit.

"Wolves," I said.

"Good," the customs man said. "We need 'em here in Ontario." I did not know whether he believed they were wolves or not, but he didn't pursue the matter, mainly because animals entering Canada were not the responsibility of the Canadian customs. This came under the jurisdiction of the Ontario Department of Lands and Forests, which didn't check you in at the border; and anyway, Phil Rhynas, a big wheel in that department and a good friend, had assured us that there would be no trouble about the wolves because they had been brought in from outside the province. They *do* have a law about "harboring" wildlife if it's strictly Ontario wildlife.

After we had cleared customs, which is so casual in a car and so careful at the airports, we settled down for a long, long, LONG drive to Chinookville, the nearest metropolis to Lost Lake, which was to be the last stop for Wolf, Lady, and their family. "Last stop"—even *that* sounded ominous to me. I was that nervous about my experiment. But I knew I had to do it. I couldn't see these lovely, intelligent animals locked up for the rest of their natural lives. The chances were greater in the woods. Much greater. But a risky, dangerous freedom would be better than a safe prison.

We had to time our arrival in Chinookville to coincide with daylight because the Canada Goose Airways people didn't believe in flying at night, and rightly so—they had no instruments or lights for landing in the pitch black waters of some northern lake.

This disadvantage meant that we had to spend one night on the road in a motel. There are plenty of motels all along the Trans Canada Highway, but very few, we found, that had the welcome sign out for wolf families. Not that we mentioned the wolves when we went in to register. We didn't have to. Immediately, or I should say a few moments, after we stopped in front of a motel

131

office and were just about to sign the register, all the wolves, who were crowded together in a large special cage in the back of the station wagon. would—as on a downbeat—launch into the most mournful chorus ever heard this side of the Wailing Wall at the Chevy plant in Detroit the day of the big recall. The motel clerk would stop short—his magic pen motionless in midair.

"What's that?" was the standard question.

"Wolves," was the standard answer.

Get back in the car and leave was the standard procedure.

Finally, the wolves, who were getting just as worn out as we were, missed their cue as we stopped at one of those "last chance" motels, and they were quiet as we signed in and were given the key to cabin number thirteen—which *may* have been a coincidence. At exactly twelve midnight, which was just a few minutes after we had all wearily thrown ourselves in our lumpy, mildew smelling beds. the downbeat came, and Wolf, Lady, and their five howling offspring attacked the first blood-curdling note of the wolf version of "Onward Christian Soldiers"—with some counterpoint which sounded like "Glory, Glory, Hallelujah" as sung by seven Robert Merrills with his testicles caught in a Mixmaster.

The cause we don't know, but the effect was immediate. Fifteen minutes later, I found myself by myself parked under the deep-black starbright Canadian sky in a large open field—far from the madding crowd but awful close to my seven wolves, all outdoing themselves in seven separate lullabies, all guaranteed to defeat any effect of the four Seconals I had downed under the false impression that they would carry me across the threshold into Dreamland. Reiko, Bobby. and Timothy were still at the motel sleeping like little indifferent angels. The motel man said *they* could stay—if they didn't howl.

It was a long night. The longest night of my life. And in the morning my eyes didn't even blink. For the rest of the day I stared like a stuffed owl.

"Papa looks funny," Bobby said, as we once again continued north toward Lost Lake.

"I didn't sleep *all* night," I said.

132

"Gee," Bobby said. "We slept fine—but first we watched television, didn't we, Mamma?"

"Yes," Reiko said. "They had a good movie. It was in color—"

"Yeah," Bobby said. "It was about this man, see—he was building this log cabin up in the woods, see—he wanted this girl to marry him and live in this cabin, see—this was long ago, see—and all the while he was building the cabin, wolves were surrounding him and howling, see— Gee, they had a lot of wolves in this movie —and, boy, did they ever *howl!* You shoulda seen it, Papa."

I turned my unblinking eyes on him, and before I could say anything, Bobby edged away from me.

"Gee, Papa." he said, in a voice just a little above a whisper. "What did I *say?*"

"Don't talk to Papa when he's driving," Reiko said. "Papa's nervous."

"Can I sit back there with you?" Bobby asked. Reiko agreed to this and I was left all alone with my unblinking, laser-beam eyes—staring deep into the future, the past, and sideways.

We reached Chinookville with very little daylight time to spare for flying to Lost Lake, and Charlie Burke, the Canada Goose Airways chief pilot. wasn't too anxious to fly us and our cargo of now-indifferent wolves. They were indifferent because they were in the last stages of exhaustion. Between the howling, the discomfort created by motion sickness, and anxiety, they had abandoned themselves to their fate. Almost. As soon as I started to transfer them from the car cage to the airplane cage they became very active and unruly. I had to have everyone clear the dock, because the wolves were spooked by the strangers, and take each animal, one by one, into the plane. I felt like Noah loading a cargo of unwilling passengers who would rather stay and drown than take their chances in such a weird-looking ark.

Lady and her five pups were fairly tractable. but Wolf was something else. I had to first get him out of the car cage with its narrow door. Every time I would try

133

he'd brace himself with his two huge front paws against the sides of the cage door. I doubt if a tractor could have pulled him through it in this attitude, so I had to try strategy. The only strategy I could think of was a three-pound fryer. I held this up to him, and he guardedly inspected it. As he was doing this with his long wolf nose, I drew the chicken carcass out an inch at a time away from the cage. When he finally put his head entirely outside the cage, I gave a tremendous yank on the heavy chain leash, which was attached to the double choke collars he wore, and he came flying out of the car cage and onto the dock. Forgetting all about the tempting morsel with which I had been enticing him. Now he was surrounded by a world of danger. The airplane rubbing against the old auto tire buffers along the dock squealed slightly, causing Wolf to attempt a dash for freedom. But he didn't know which way freedom was, for he was surrounded by all the everyday items associated with the world of the bush pilot. Stacks of oil drums. Two gasoline pumps, looking to a wolf like tall men with one long arm each. Cars were also parked on the dock, and boxes and cartons, and lumber and rolls of wire, plus iron pipe, and stacks of shingles, and the Canadian maple leaf flag flapping in the breezes. This last was very unnerving to Wolf, and I had to drag him under it to get to the plane ramp and the other cage. This took me a full fifteen minutes and every bit of strength I had left after long years of strenuous typing. The ramp up into the plane was familiar to me, but this time it looked narrower, and when I finally got Wolf on it, it had more spring than a trampoline. It was like walking a tightrope that had suddenly turned into a rubber band. Midway to the plane door Wolf slipped off the ramp and fell into the water—away from the dock and on the inside of the plane's right pontoon. I don't know how he did it, but he did. This panicked him entirely, but it also *bewildered* him, and by wrapping the chain leash around a piece of steel that was holding the plane and the pontoon together I inched him bit by bit up out of the water and onto the ramp and into the cage on the plane. I had shortened my life by a couple of years, but I had him safely aboard. Now all I had left to do was get him off the plane at Lost Lake. Took two Alka-Seltzers.

28

WE arrived at Lost Lake on the last day of August, which wasn't the most suitable date because Bobby was supposed to start attending the Honansville elementary school on September 3. This didn't allow much time to train our wolves to be independent and self-supporting. But this couldn't be helped because the wolf pups were *over* four months old, and I felt it would soon be now or never for them. Starting on September 3, Bobby would be tutored by *me* in my best Prussian general fashion. This hadn't worked when we were living at Lost Lake permanently, but we were all older now and I knew that Bobby, who had his whole life before him, would not suffer too much losing a couple of months of schooling. With the wolves, their schooling would have to be brief and to the point, and they would have to graduate before the weather got too severe—which could happen in the north any time after September.

When we had gotten settled in our comfortable peeled-spruce lodge, unpacked all of our Hudson's Bay blankets, and checked on our stockpiles of white birch firewood, which were stashed all around the lake in inconvenient places where it had been cut, I took all of the wolves over to one of the larger islands in Lost Lake. This island was some distance away from our home base and therefore was not as safe from hunters as I would have liked, but the island did have some wildlife—rabbits, mice, red squirrels, chipmunks, plus an immense beaver house adjoining the large rock formation in the west side of the island. There were plenty of beaver in Lost Lake, so I assumed the beaver house was occupied.

There was no cozy wooden wolf den on the island, but there were several nice caves. They were not very big or deep, but I felt they would make dandy dens in this transitional period.

As soon as I released Wolf, Lady, and the five pups, who were now quite large and finally looked like wolves, they all stood close to me and the boat cage I had used to bring them to the island. They couldn't quite believe it or trust it. They were, for the first time, unsurrounded by steel wire fencing. Wolf, as the head of the family, moved first. He started to sniff out the territory nearest him. Then Lady and the pups followed his example. Soon they were branching out in all directions, covering every bit of ground inch by inch. To a wolf nothing is too minute to be investigated. The thoroughness of their exhaustive examination made their progress slow; they took hours, it seemed, to sniff around and analyze the deep, hidden meaning of an ancient pile of moose droppings. After they had diagnosed this particular problem, they started to rub their necks in it. It was quite a sight—seven wolves, apparently in ecstasy, rubbing themselves silly in a mound of moose manure. After several minutes, Wolf stood up and, seemingly realizing suddenly how free he was, started dashing around and through the underbrush, startling snowshoe rabbits and chipmunks and a few ruffed grouse into hysteria. Wolf didn't even notice them. He was free! And that was all that mattered. To me, too.

Lady and the pups also took off through the brush, while Reiko and Bobby and Timothy and I waited near the boat and ate some sandwiches.

"They look so pretty now," Reiko said, which was probably the most complimentary thing she had ever said about a wolf. Poor Reiko. I think she wanted to love these fascinating animals as much as I did, but she was afraid. Either afraid because of childhood fairy tales which had been driven deep into her subconscious and her conscious in Japan, or afraid because they were so powerful and fierce-looking—to her. This is the reaction

136

to most people; even a wolf in complete repose with its wonderfully beautiful head snuggled down between its paws frightens them. I have always wondered why. Is it because they know it's a wolf and the very name conjures up the picture we have all seen of slavering beasts chasing a troika filled with screaming men and women and children across the frozen Russian steppes? Or a fierce painting of Remington's depicting an Indian with a tomahawk fighting off the attack of a wolf who is much bigger than the Indian—either, according to what the artist painted, the wolf had been taking vitamins, or the Indian was a dwarf, or the artist had been drinking. Both pictures are, of course, drawn from pure imagination but all too real to two generations brought up in the Wonderful World of Disney.

I have never felt the slightest fear of wolves, and I can't explain this, because I too was exposed in my pre-puberty years to all the current sadistic fairy tales. But from the time I can remember, all wild animals were lovely creatures. I wanted to hug them all—even the ones I couldn't get my chubby little arms around. I think most children are born with this love, but adults soon bat this silly notion out of their foolish little heads. My Mother and Dad were not like this—they may have read us the same exciting, if somewhat inaccurate, fairy tales, but they also loved animals, and I guess this rubbed off on me. But where I picked up my affection for the wolf is something I cannot answer. I don't even remember when it started. I think it was always there. I'm just grateful that I didn't develop a long-lasting, high-plane ardency for the Grizzly.

"Reiko," I said, "they always looked pretty. You never really tried to picture them as anything but something in a cage that had to be fed every day."

"Wolf did shi-shi in the house!" Reiko said quickly and, I thought, with a slight twinge of guilt.

"You can't housebreak a wolf," I said, "and, besides, how many hundreds of times did Bobby, and now Timothy, do shi-shi—in the house—on the carpet—on the couch—in the crib—under the crib—through the crib and over the crib!"

137

"You can't expect a baby——" Reiko started, as Bobby jumped in, "I never did shi-shi except in the toilet!"

"Bobby," I said, "you didn't even *hit* the toilet until just last week!"

"That's a goddamn lie," Bobby, who had acquired his father's extensive vocabulary, said.

"Goddamn——lie," Timothy said through his lollipop.

"You shut up!" Bobby said to Timothy.

"Bobby," Reiko said, *"you* are *ten years old* and *Timothy* is only *two*—why do *you* tell *him* to *shut up?"*

"Because," Bobby yelled, "he's always saying what I say! He bugs me!"

"Jesus Christ!" I said.

"Jesus——Christ," Timothy said, this time removing his lollipop.

"You see!" Bobby screamed.

"Shut up!" I screamed back, but like a New York cab driver with a flat on a rainy day.

This brought Wolf and Lady and the five pups back in a hurry. They were all panting heavily, their pink tongues hanging down for yards. They had been having a ball, and oh how I wished it would always be this way. Again, I said a little prayer, which had become habit-forming of late. I wanted so much for this tiny band of "predators" to live a long, happy, healthy, and wonderful life.

The pups, who now weighed about thirty-five or forty pounds, formed almost a perfect circle around Timothy as he played with his bulldozer in the mound of moose droppings. I had never allowed Timothy in the cage with them when they were confined because I thought they might scare him if he had no exit. Now surrounded by these newly wild wolves, he still had no exit, but it wasn't the same, and the wolf pups weren't the same either—they weren't nearly as rambunctious and rough as they had been in the pen. They now acted more like friendly domesticated dogs—like friendly domesticated dogs would act with any little boy. They all seemed to want him to be *their* little boy. Timothy was very casual about the whole thing—like he had spent his whole life in a mound of moose manure surrounded by five wolves. He played with his bulldozer, which wasn't making much of a dent in the mound, and talked to the wolf pups. "Nice wolfies," he said. "Dancer, Prancer, Dunder, Blitzen—" he was *naming* them, and very well, after another group, but then he got stuck and started over: "Dancer, Prancer, Dunder, Blitzen, and—and—Wolfie!"

"That's cute," Reiko said. Until then she had been concerned for Timothy. "Dancer, Prancer, Dunder, Blitzen, and Wolfie. That's cute. Let's call them that."

"Yeah," Bobby said. "That's good, Mommie—Dancer, Prancer, Dunder, Blitzen, and Wolfie!"

"It's a little late in the day to start naming them, isn't it?" I suggested.

"No," Reiko said. "It's going to be a couple of months or so before we can let them go into the big woods by themselves. They might as well have names."

"Okay with me," I said.

Timothy started in again, this time poking his little bulldozer at each wolf pup in turn: "Dancer, Prancer—"

And now Reiko, Bobby, and I joined in: "—Dunder, Blitzen, and Wolfie!"

29

WE had been at Lost Lake about a month when it started to turn cold. A few times the skies looked snowy, but it didn't snow. It just threatened. Or maybe it "warned." Everything was working fine. The generators which we depended on for light and power for the pumps and radiophone had not missed a beat. Charlie Burke flew up with supplies regularly, and the wolves were getting along beautifully in their new environment. They were catching some of the island's small game now, but because we couldn't expect them to harvest enough to live on, we augmented their wild diet with Alpo, Burgerbits, and raw chicken backs. They all looked magnificent, and their bodies had hardened considerably. Wolf's and Lady's muscles felt like steel springs, and the pups had toughened up, too. And so far we hadn't seen or heard any hunters.

I was very pleased that Wolf and Lady seemed to be able to hunt almost as if they had been in the wilds since birth, but of course all they had caught was very small, both in the amount of nourishment and the effort it took to bring down a rabbit or a squirrel. If they were going to exist and survive in the future in the deep woods, they would have to kill much larger animals, like moose and deer. I couldn't let them go into the woods and expect them to learn this special technique instantaneously, so the problem was would they be able to subsist long enough on rabbits, mice, and other small animals while they learned what it was like to face a moose or ambush a deer? And how long would it take them to learn that they could never possibly take a full-grown adult moose unless it was very old or very sick? And they would also have to find out the hard way that they could never outrun a deer—that is, a deer that was not very old, or very young, or injured. They would have to learn the wolf method of surprise and ambush. I only could hope that all this would be instinctive. I had no reason to believe that it wouldn't be, but the very thought of my lovely Wolf, Lady, and Dancer, Prancer, Dunder, Blitzen, and Wolfie dying of starvation in the bitter cold of a northern Ontario winter gave me great pause.

I had no choice, I realized. When the time came for them to be released into this inhospitable (unless you are prepared) north country, I would just have to let them go and hope and pray.

And the burden, just as with humans, was on the parents to supply enough food until the pups were old enough to hunt on their own, which would occur sometime when they were ten months old or more. They would have their second teeth, and if they had watched their parents carefully enough, they would, by imitation —and, I hoped, by instinct—know just what it takes to live off the country. Wolf style.

Toward the end of October the air was a bit more than nippy. Ice had started its tentative formation on the lake, but still no snow had fallen. Ordinarily I loved snow, and so did Reiko and Bobby. Timothy seemed to have been born with his affection and fascination with snow. Before he was two years old, we had to bolt all the doors or we'd notice the sudden quiet inside the house. We then knew that Timothy would be outside gamboling in the fluffy white stuff. Sometimes this gamboling took place in the nude. I took sneaky photos of him once. He looked just like an elfin snowdrop. There may be no such thing as an elfin snowdrop, but that's what he looks like in the pictures. But we were happy that it had not snowed so far at Lost Lake, because it would have hampered our care and feeding of the wolves on the big island. With my knowledge of the northern Canadian weather, I was sure the snow would come at the *wrong moment*—just as we were *halfway* between our lodge and the wolf island, as we put-putted through the thin ice with a boatload of food for the animals. If this happened we would instantly lose our sense of direction; all water and ice looks alike, with no point of reference. Eventually we would bump into some piece of land that would give us a clue to our whereabouts. But the wolves might not be fed for quite some time because the snowstorm might last quite some time. This was all right for wild wolves, because the records show that they can go a long while without food, but for our wolves no food—and no Big Brother showing up at the right time—might be a traumatic experience. And for me. I was getting so edgy about the whole experiment I did not think *clearly*. A feat I have difficulty with when conditions are perfect.

I almost went off the deep end entirely when "The Hunter" showed up.

The Hunter arrived one night just as we were sitting down to dinner. It was already dark and there was no moon. There was a knock on the door. This startled all of us into silence. We just sat and stared at nothing. Who would be knocking on the front door of a log house sixty miles from the nearest neighbor? At six o'clock at night? I reached for my .38 police special, which I kept hanging beside the fireplace, and cautiously opened the door. Don't ask why I kept a .38 police special hanging beside the fireplace—because I don't know why. I've just lived this way all of my life—waiting to be attacked. Someday, if I can find a cut-rate psychiatrist, I'll ask *him* why.

"Who is it?" Reiko asked. The sound of her voice startled me, and I cocked the pistol. It was a reflex action and I didn't have to do it. Standing on the other side of the door, shivering in the late October chill, was the sorriest looking skid-row bum I have ever seen. He looked like a skid-row bum, but he was carrying the biggest gun I have ever seen. They must have had a sale at Navarone, because this gun couldn't have come from anywhere else.

"I saw your light," the skid-row bum said.

"Yeah," I said. "We—we put it on when it's dark."

"Who is it?" Reiko still wanted to know.

"I'm a hunter, Ma'am," the skid-row bum said, walking into the living room, and into the light, without any invitation. Not that I would have turned anyone away, but I would have liked to ask him if he'd like to come in. "I've been hunting up here for years," he said.

"You ought to go home once in a while," I said, trying to be jolly. "You know—rest up a bit."

The Hunter didn't appreciate my jocular innuendo —for him it was perfectly natural to look like a skid-row bum. His Mackinaw was ripped in a half dozen places. His fur cap was moth-eaten down to just plain fuzz. The knees of his corduroy pants were worn as thin as Kleenex. He wore boots which must have been the first pair ever made after Firestone discovered that if you mix sulphur with rubber you get something which can be made into rubber boots without cracking to pieces in the winter and melting in the summer. He wore no gloves, and his hands looked like two raw cargo hooks. He also wore glasses—*thick* glasses which made his reddish-blue eyes look like they were under water. And he was scraggly. So scraggly, I didn't think there was anything under his clothes except a few wire coat hangers held together with paper clips.

"What are you hunting?" I asked, in order to keep the conversation on some subject which was indigenous to his social stratum.

"Deer," The Hunter said.

"Would you like-a tea?" Reiko said, using the only gambit she ever learned to steer anyone from any unpleasantness. But it didn't work. Not this time, anyway.

"Deer!" I said, louder than I had intended. "This isn't the deer season!"

"I know," The Hunter said, "but we gotta have meat on the table."

"What's the matter with the A & P?" I asked, in a strictly noncongenial host tone. The Hunter looked blank at this.

"We don't have any meat on *our* table," Bobby said. He sounded unfriendly, too, because he was at last beginning to assume some of the righteous indignations of his old man. But he was correct—there was no meat on the table this particular night—just noodles, rice wrapped in nori (seaweed, which is delicious), fried octopus (which is delicious), and a huge bowl of soup (what kind I don't know—the ingredients are something mysteriously Oriental, but also delicious).

"Would you like-a dinner?" Reiko asked, like a Geisha girl who hadn't had a customer for ages.

"Yes," The Hunter said. "I been hunting all day. Kinda gives a man an appetite."

"Not many deer left around here," I said, still bristling inwardly at this bastard's bland attitude toward Ontario's conservation laws.

"No," The Hunter said, leaning his enormous rifle against the wall and pulling up a chair. "The goddamn wolves get most of them."

I had to wait for a moment before I replied to this. I took a deep breath and said, "Not many goddamn wolves left around here."

"There's a few," The Hunter said, slurping huge slurps of Reiko's delicious mystery soup. "But we'll soon get rid of them."

143

"Gee," Bobby started to say, "I hope you don't——"

I interrupted quickly with, "You know George Elson?" I spoke of the district game warden.

"That sonofabitch!" The Hunter said. Then to Reiko, "Beggin' your pardon, Ma'am."

"What for?" Reiko wanted to know. She had heard "sonofabitch" so often in her years with me she thought it was a standard American word like "Minutemaid" or "McDonald's."

"You mean George Elson is a sonofabitch because he tries to enforce the game laws?"

"He tries to keep decent folk from killing a deer when they want to."

"Christ!" I said, getting hot. "If everybody killed a deer when they felt like it there wouldn't be *any* left!" I started shoveling the nori-wrapped rice into my mouth to control myself a little. It didn't work too well.

"It's those goddamn wolves," The Hunter said. "They're the ones responsible for the deer shortage. They kill just for the sport of it. They're born killers——"

"Last year," I said, quietly, and in a tone I hoped was sinister, and believable, "last year, George Elson told me there were so many hunters up here killing the deer that from *his* plane it looked like the invasion of Normandy."

"That sonofabitch!" The Hunter said.

30

FOR the next three days after The Hunter left our reluctant hospitality to knock off his illegal deer —if he could find any after last year's "harvest"—I took my little tent and my goose-down sleeping bag and stayed on the island where the wolves were, now more apprehensive than ever about letting them loose on the mainland. I thought of abandoning the whole plan and hauling them back to Honansville and the wolf pen, but the thought of these seven beautiful creatures locked in the confines—no matter how large—of a pen saddened me to the point of melancholia. I just couldn't do it. I thought maybe, after our brief encounter with the backwoods bigot with the thick glasses and the big gun, we had chosen the wrong place to set them free. I thought maybe Minnesota would be the answer, because I understood that they had at last removed the bounty paid for dead wolves. But then I learned they had not placed the few that were left under the protection of the endangered species law, so the removal of the paying of blood money did very little for the Minnesota wolves.

"Maybe we could take them up to some national park where they allow wolves," Reiko said. This was a good suggestion, but I had contacted the guardians of every bit of the precious ground of wildlife refuges in the United States and Canada, and none of these places needed any more wolves. Or wanted any. So the whole thing was up to us. (Incidentally, look at a map of the United States and Canada sometime and try to find the wildlife refuges. You'll have to have pretty good eyesight and a large magnifying glass. The wildlife refuges are there, but in all of the vast wildernesses of the United States and Canada, the areas given over to wildlife protection are infinitesimal. Mere pinpoints—like Man in the ages of this earth.)

"There are no places that want wolves," I told Reiko.

"Well," she said, surprising me because she wasn't too fond of our isolation of the moment, without going *farther* afield, "why don't we go up to some of those places you're always talking about, like the Yukon, or the Northwest Territories, or maybe even some far place in Alaska?" I was touched by Reiko's warm concern, but it was not practical. Any place we chose would have to be investigated so thoroughly that the time it would take would make it impossible just to transport the wolves to what we might pick as a safer haven. The pups were getting very big and would never all fit into any station wagon and/or a bush plane, unless we took them two at a time. But that would defeat our purpose of releasing them as a group so they'd stand a better chance

145

all together as a hunting pack. So we were stuck, if that was the word, with our original plan. We could just trust to luck—the wolves' luck, not ours, unfortunately. I was beginning to feel like I wished it were me who would be going into a strange, new, dangerous world. Maybe for the first time I was beginning to feel like a father—even if my children were seven timber wolves.

31

THE time was drawing close to November, when we intended to release the wolves into the woods. The weather was very cold now, but clear; the wolves had nice thick, warm coats, and they all looked enormous. Even the pups, who were almost six months old, looked like adults. My God, they were beautiful!

We had forgotten all about the moth-eaten hunter who stayed with us that one night. We had almost forgotten the rest of the world entirely—which *used* to be considered antisocial.

The ice on Lost Lake was a tiny bit thicker but nowhere near thick enough to walk on or stop the progress of our outboard motorboat to and from Wolf Island. The days were clear, and the forests smelled smoky—I don't know why, there were no fires anywhere—and the nights were fantastic. The stars, as everyone always says, looked like you could reach up and touch them. They were a hundred times brighter than they are in Honansville or anywhere near any electrified community. And the nights were very quiet except for the whispery creaking of our docks and the tiny lapping sounds of water and ice meeting. I thought, *Why* can't we stay here for *always? What* is there anywhere *else?* I couldn't think of *anything.*

The lovely, soothing, and healing peace of Lost Lake was shattered by the twin motors of Charlie Burke's

146

Otter, a much larger plane than he usually piloted. It landed smoothly on the upper end of Lost Lake and taxied for a mile or so to our airplane dock. We thought Charlie was just dropping by to see if we were all right, because we hadn't ordered anything from Chinookville, but this wasn't the case at all. Charlie brought us a big surprise. The Honansville Ecology Group—en masse. Harry and Ruthie Mitchell. Frank and Ethel Krasselt. Virgil Palmquist and Reggie Mailer. Bella Brown, who looked Neanderthal in her old muskrat fur coat. And Rogers and Alice Dotson, who were dressed like the first Byrd expedition. We had hit the jackpot!

Almost immediately, after the first flush of surprise and delight at seeing this ill-mixed crowd, my Nietzsche-oriented mind envisioned our generators exploding, never to run again, and all of us being stranded—marooned—abandoned forever by the outside world, and after the food ran out—eating each other! A horrible thought, indeed, but tempered with the comforting thought that, on Bella Brown alone, we could all live for months.

"You got a lot of friends," Charlie Burke said to me as I escorted him back to his plane after a quick cup of coffee.

"You think so?" Then I asked him to check up on us once in a while.

"Don't you worry about Old Charlie," he said.

"I'm not worried about Old Charlie," I said. "I'm worried about getting stuck—forever—with my friends."

"You don't like your friends?" Charlie asked.

"Yes," I said, "but not three times a day." Charlie didn't comment on this. He just looked at me for a long look, then climbed up into the plane and taxied to the center of the lake and took off. As he zoomed low over the house I saw something flutter down from the plane. It took me a half hour to find it, but it was worth the time. It was a little card that read "Peace." The card was attached by a bit of string to a live 30.06 rifle bullet. For weight?

By the time I got back to the living room everyone had gotten over their "ohs" and "ahs" about what a lovely spot we had and had settled down to "relaxing," with Reiko very busy mixing the relaxers.

"How did you ever *find* this place?" Harry Mitchell wanted to know, as usual gesturing and slopping his martini over everything within striking distance that was absorbent—which included his red suede vest and Alice Dotson's hand-knitted Yugoslavian poncho.

"Christ, Harry!" Alice Dotson said, not too disturbed.

"How did *you* ever find this place?" I countered.

"We just asked the bush pilot to take us to Hansel and Gretel's, and he knew right away what we meant."

"Yeah," I said, "we use that name when we buy anything on *time* in Chinookville—makes us easy to find in case we miss a payment."

"Oh, I *adore* this place," Virgil Palmquist gushed. "And those *trees!*—those *lovely, large, gorgeous* trees!—they're so *old*—they *must* be *antiques!*"

Then Virgil screamed to his partner, "Reggie—*look!* Look at those *marvelous* antique rocks over *there!*"

"Oh, I know," Reggie Mailer screamed back. "I *love* them! I love every *rock* and *rill!* If only we could take some of those rocks back to the shop. They'd sell like hot cakes in Connecticut!"

I failed to see why rocks would sell like hot cakes in Connecticut, which is nothing but rocks, but Reggie was so enthused, and shrill, I didn't want to kill his enthusiasm or his shrillity. I knew that deep down inside that homely faggot there was a beautiful mezzo-soprano trying to get out.

Frank and Ethel Krasselt were conferring on *what* to *paint* first. I would have liked to suggest the *outside* of the lodge. The shellac, or whatever someone had put on there a few years before, was peeling like a stripper trying to get everything off before the raid.

Rogers and Alice Dotson had settled themselves nicely. Alice was busy sipping her double brandy and wringing out her Yugoslavian poncho, while Rogers Dotson was at his ease with his drink, his horrific meerschaum pipe, and his continual stroking of a nonexistent Irish setter by his side. His nonexistent Irish setter was the most faithful nonexistent dog I've ever seen. He went everywhere with Rogers Dotson.

Bella Brown, who refused to take off her muskratty brown coat, checked and rechecked everything in the lodge. Then she looked out of every window—at least twice. Then she went to the front door, opened it, and let go with a juicy quart of Mail Pouch, just missing a little chipmunk who had come up to see what the hell all the noise was about. The chipmunk didn't believe it when he saw Bella. He knew there were no grizzlies in this part of Canada, but what else could it be? After a moment he decided he'd rather not know and ducked down the nearest escape hole.

Bella spat again and came back inside. "I'll say one thing for this place," Bella said. "You got real nice neighbors."

"We don't have *any* neighbors," Reiko said.

"I know," Bella said. "They're the best kind."

Reiko didn't quite get this, so she said, "Anybody wanna tea?" This was like asking the crew of the *Bounty* the day they arrived at Tahiti if anybody wanted to stay on board the ship.

By the time the sun dipped behind the tallest of the darkening pines, every one of our guests was pretty well zonked. Even Virgil and Reggie, who rarely had more than eight or ten drinks apiece, seemed to be moving about the living room without touching the floor. I have heard that the north does this to people. A recent article in *Time* reported everyone in Point Barrow, our northernmost city in Alaska, is a *lush,* which is not a bad idea if you live in Point Barrow. There's not much to do there, but the days just fly by.

It was too late to see the wolves, which was why the entire Honansville Ecology Group had descended on us —they said—so we had to postpone the trip to Wolf Island until the next day. I shudder to think what would have happened if someone had suggested a midnight visit. I'm sure with all the drunken motorboat driving that the name would have been changed overnight to the Honansville Survivors or the Lost Lake

149

Tragedy Group. *I* wouldn't have trusted any of them in a boat *sober*.

During the afternoon of high old times, Reiko had secretly prepared four of our guest cabins for use at least *some* part of the night. She counted on them getting tired after a while, but she and I both missed the estimated time by several hours. When the party finally broke up I had to first guide the married couples to their cabins. Then I took Virgil, Reggie, and Bella to our largest guest cabin. I hung a sheet across the room like *It Happened One Night*, separating Bella from Virgil and Reggie.

"What the hell is *that* for?" Bella demanded.

"Privacy," I said, in a small voice.

"Whose?" Bella said. "Theirs or mine?"

"Don't you remember *It Happened One Night* with Clark Gable?" I said.

"Not with *me*, it didn't," Bella said, with a trace of alcoholic wistfulness in her raspy voice.

"That Clark Gable!" Virgil trilled. "He was really *something*! He was a *man!*"

"What do you think *I* am?" Reggie answered, teasing his Prince Valiant hairdo with a sequined comb as he prepared for the slumber hour.

"Bunk beds!" Virgil shrieked as he suddenly became aware of that section of the decor. "Bunk beds!" he repeated an octave higher. "Reggie! We're going to be separated! Can you *bear* it!"

"I'll kill myself first," Reggie said.

"How?" Bella wanted to know. Then she added, "And when?"

"Look," I said to Reggie, being very sober and very tired, "if you want to kill yourself the *easy* way, don't *turn off* those propane gas lights. Just *blow* them out and go to bed."

"Will you put flowers every Sunday on my lonely little grave high on a windy hill?" he asked.

"Yes," I said. "Antique plastic flowers—I'll buy them at your shop—from Virgil."

"Promise?"

"Promise."

150

Bella lifted up the dividing sheet I had hung and spat on their side of the cabin floor. They both leaped, shrieking, into the lower bunk bed as I left.

The sun was just pinking the eastern sky and the loons were starting their first unearthly callings of the day. The eerie sounds of the loons were duplicated in my stomach and in my head. I raised my eyes to the heavens and prayed that the generators would not fail us and that Charlie Burke would come back when he said he would. I loved the Honansville Ecology Group —but only if I knew they were going home again. So far, although it was only the first day, no one had mentioned anything resembling a date of departure. I hoped it would be soon after they had visited Wolf Island. I had work to do, and plans to make, and I didn't want to be chained to my "perfect host" role. I can be a "perfect host" for no longer than three hours and forty-six minutes (I've been timed by John Cameron Swayze). After that I become schizoid, idiopathic, and catatonic. All of which adds up to I am not much fun at the Harvest Moon Ball.

32

IT was noon before we got everybody up and fed and into the boats for the journey to Wolf Island. I venture to guess that Magellan had less trouble getting things organized for his first world cruise. We had to use three boats to accommodate the Honansville group, which meant that Bobby, who was just ten, had to pilot one of them. It was his first time (which *I* didn't tell anyone—*he* did), but he managed very well— hardly scraping any of the many rocky reefs we had all over Lost Lake. Reiko and I drove the other two boats, and I appointed Timothy, who was almost three, as first mate. He didn't know what it was, but no one else did either so it worked out fine.

The trip to Wolf Island took longer than usual because the boats were a little overloaded and a brisk wind kept scooping water and ice into them, which made everyone except Harry Mitchell and his semilovely wife, Ruthie, apprehensive. Harry and Ruthie had no faith in bacon and eggs in the morning. They placed their trust in vodka and tonic. And on a trip such as we were now undertaking, I can't fault them for this. I would have liked to have been more than a little unaware of the perils of the deep. There were not enough life jackets to go around, and even if there were, it would have taken hours to get them on everybody. A hangover does not add to one's proficiency when it comes to the intricacies of tying a simple overhead knot or the ability to tell which is the *front* of the bright-orange kapok-stuffed safety garments. I was almost grateful that we were short of life-saving equipment, and it wouldn't have mattered much anyway, I don't think; if there had been an upsetting or a sinking, no one could last very long in the now-freezing water.

Wolf Island was a large disappointment to all concerned. Wolf, Lady, and the five large pups were spooked into hiding by this large crowd of noisy Honansvillites—as I knew they would be—and were nowhere to be seen.

After we landed, only Bella Brown and Alice Dotson got their feet wet, slipping as they descended from the boat to the shore of the island, and sloshed around noisily looking for the wolves. The island wasn't that large that the wolves could hide completely and all at one time, but the vegetation was thick and the many caves made it a little easier for them to avoid us almost completely. Only occasionally as they switched from cover to cover did we see anything of them, and then it was usually only the flick of a bushy gray tail or a furtively curious wolf face.

Virgil and Reggie started to complain—or bitch, I guess would be a better word.

"My God," Virgil said, with a new resonance he seemed to have picked up since he arrived in the woods, "we fly a thousand miles up here to this uninhabited

152

planet to see a new wolf pack, and what do we see—nothing but blueberry bushes, rocks, trees, and red squirrels. We can see all this in Honansville—and we don't have to freeze our asses off doing it!"

"Yes," Bella Brown agreed, "my ass is about to drop off!"

"Good God!" Reggie said. "Don't let that happen! It'll tip the whole island!"

"How would you like a good belt right in the mouth?" Bella said, coming right to the point.

"Oh, go shoe a horse!" Reggie said, with more guts than I thought he had.

"Anybody wanna tea?" Reiko said, although we were far, far from a kitchen and a teapot.

"Look," I said to the disheveled and disappointed ensemble, "the wolves are just too scared to show themselves. They just don't remember seeing so many people before."

"We used to come and look at them when they were pups in Honansville," Rogers Dotson said, sitting on a fallen cedar log, puffing away on his polluted meerschaum, and stroking his imaginary Irish setter (I resolved then and there that someday I would slip a dog under his stroking hand just to see his reaction—he might not even notice, or he might drop dead—it depended on how quickly he could adjust to changing conditions).

"When you visited them in Honansville the pups were just about three months old. Wolf pups at that age have no trouble making friends, but after a while they change and usually they only trust the members of the immediate family."

"I wouldn't trust *my* immediate family," Harry Mitchell said, and his semilovely wife, Ruthie, laughed.

"After that age they are extremely wary—especially of adult males," I said.

"Then we'd better get off the island," Virgil said to Reggie. Ruthie laughed again.

"Maybe," I said, trying to save the day, "maybe if we all got back into the boats, then circled the island slowly and quietly—maybe they'll show themselves."

"Why don't you stay here while we all circle?" Reiko said. "Try to get them out into the open with some dog biscuits." She handed me a large box with the picture of Lassie on the side of it.

"Okay," I said. "It's worth a try."

"We'd love to paint the wolves," Ethel Krasselt said. "Wouldn't we, Frank?"

"Yeah," Frank said. "Maybe we could get Pegeen Fitzgerald down in Kent to hang them in her store—she's got a lot of great paintings there."

I let Frank and Ethel have their pipe dream. How the hell they expected to paint the wolves if they never came out of the bush was something that didn't occur to them.

The embarking from Wolf Island was just as tedious as it was from our home dock, only this time there was no dock and a helluva lot of wet feet were created in a relatively short time. But finally they were all in the boats and they started to circle the island slowly, while I turned with my box of dog biscuits to try to entice Wolf, Lady, and their rough-and-ready brood out into the open near that landing place. I knew this would take some doing and a lot of patience—and I *could* be patient with *wolves*.

I could hear the boats slowly cruising around the island on the far side as I called to the wolves, or I should say I called Wolf, who knew me longer and better than the others. A half hour passed and nothing happened. I called. I entreated. I pleaded. I howled like a wolf. I would have liked to have a movie of what I was doing—all by myself in a small open place on an island in the middle of a wilderness lake sitting on my haunches—howling. Who would believe this was a sane person? Not even my mother.

I was about to give up the whole thing, and so were the people in the boats, I suspected, when I noticed one bush moving, while the bushes surrounding it were lifeless. I cooed some wolf talk (which I had made up over the years) and waved a handful of dog biscuits at the bush. Wolf came out, carefully and ready to duck back into safety if he had to. He moved on steel springs.

154

The hair along his spine was raised, and he didn't look friendly.

"Come on, Boy," I said. "Everything is okay. Everybody's gone." I'm sure he didn't believe this because he could hear the throttled-down outboard motors on the other side of the island just as clearly as I could—or I should say, a lot clearer. A wolf has a supersonic built-in radar.

The hair on his back lay down flat again as he came to me and snatched a mouthful of dog biscuits from my extended hand. He ground them to powder instantly and swallowed them and looked for more. I had a full box of dog biscuits, but I felt I should ration them a little now so I'd have enough for the rest of the pack, so I only gave him one biscuit this time. I think he swallowed it whole. At that moment the boats came around the point and Wolf started to dive for cover, but as I reassured him, and the people in the boats were quiet as they glided by, he changed his mind and ate another biscuit—never once taking his eyes off the boats and their bizarre crews. I motioned to Reiko that the boats should go around once more. I felt reasonably sure that by that time Lady and her pups would come out of hiding and join in the dog biscuit feast. It wasn't too long after the boats had passed and were out of sight that Lady and the pups did just that, and I was soon up to my dog biscuit box in playfully snapping and jumping wolves. They made it very difficult to maintain my balance and dole out the dog biscuits so each one got his or her fair share. I was breaking them in half now to make them last until the boats came around again.

As soon as the boats came into view around the point all the fun went out of the biscuit party for the wolves. They all stood stock still. They might have been statues if you didn't know. All seven pairs of amber eyes followed the progress of the boats, but they didn't run away. I tried to keep feeding them, as if nothing out of the ordinary was happening, but this didn't work. Nobody was hungry anymore.

Everything was serene, but tense. The wolves looked

155

enormous and beautiful in that little clearing surrounded by tall pines and spruce, with occasional clusters of white birch for contrast. It was a picture I will never forget. Then Virgil, who had become bored with the shoreline of the island and had been gazing at a far-off bank of snow clouds, turned and suddenly saw the wolf tableau on the shore. He let go with a shrieking, screaming whoop that would have startled Paul Bunyan's great blue ox, and the wolves were gone. Like they were never there.

No one spoke to Virgil for the rest of that day and most of that night, including his partner, Reggie.

After dinner, when the brandy had been passed around several times, Virgil said, "I think you're *all shits,* and *you,*" he said, pointing a long finger at Reggie, "you're a *double* shit!" Then he threw open the front door and stalked off into night. There was a long, quiet pause after this, broken only by the sounds of brandy sniffing and swirling. Finally Reggie said, "What's a *double* shit?"

I waited for Reiko to suggest tea, but she was silent this time. Maybe she knew it was hopeless, or maybe we had run out of tea.

"Speaking of whores," Harry Mitchell said, "I remember once in Butte, Montana——" That was as far as he got when Reggie jumped up, rushed over to Harry, and grabbed him by the lapels. Harry didn't resist but he spilled *all* of his martini.

"You know what you are, Harry Mitchell," Reggie yelled, right into Harry's face. "You're a *triple* shit!" Then Reggie slammed out of the room.

Harry Mitchell thought this over for a long moment, then he said—to all of us—"Does that beat two pair?"

33

TWO days after the arrival, en masse, of the Honansville Ecology Group at Lost Lake, and the day after the night of the unpleasantness between Harry Mitchell and Reggie Mailer, all was serene. Harry Mitchell remembered nothing of Reggie Mailer's sudden outburst of lacy violence, and Reggie Mailer seemed to have forgotten Harry Mitchell entirely—he was so entranced by his first wilderness experience.

It was the morning of a perfect day. The sky was a brilliant Canadian blue, which was bluer than anywhere else, and a soft but very cool breeze trailed across the surface of the lake, barely disturbing its azure waters, now diamonded by millions of tiny sheets of broken ice which mirrored the bright October sun.

"What a lovely place to study ecology," Reggie said to Alice Dotson, who was trying to bring herself back to this world over a cup of espresso, "right here in the virgin forest! This is where it all began!"

Alice Dotson looked at Reggie incomprehensively. "Where *what* all began?"

"The water, the skies, the trees, the earth!" Reggie said. He was bubbling now.

"Oh," Alice Dotson said, refilling her espresso cup and lighting the end of her amber cigarette holder.

"But where will it all end?" Rogers Dotson asked from the depths of our only comfortable chair next to the fireplace. *"Where*—will it all end?"

Before anyone could answer the unanswerable, Bobby came screaming into the house. "Papa! A plane! A plane!"

"What's so unusual about a plane?" Virgil Palmquist wanted to know. "They fly over Honansville all day long —and all night long too."

"You're a thousand miles north of Honansville now,"

I said, "and when you see a plane around here it's a big event."

"I'm thrilled," Virgil said, in a voice overflowing with ennui and torpor.

I was glad to hear about the plane, even if Virgil wasn't too moved. I thought maybe this was the plane which would take the Honansville Ecology Group back to Chinookville and home. I wanted to get on with my wolf training, such as it was, and I needed every bit of energy and concentration for it. I didn't feel I could keep up my role as the perfect host too long. At the moment I was too concerned about my wolves. People would have to be secondary in the natural order of things, until I had done what I had to do.

As its floats splashed down into Lost Lake, I could see the plane was too small to take back the Honansville group—not together anyway. By the time the little Canada Goose Airways Cessna 180 bumped its rubber bumpers against our airplane dock, *everybody* was there. Even Virgil Palmquist, who feigned great interest in his lacquered fingernails as the plane swung alongside the dock.

"Got the Shimkin family here!" Charlie Burke, Canada Goose's chief pilot, shouted down from the opened cockpit window. There were murmurs of surprise and approval from everyone in the group of welcomers. Dr. Shimkin was very popular in Honansville. I liked him, too, and greatly admired the dark beauty of his wife, Lillian. And their kids weren't half bad, either.

"Great!" I yelled back. "How are you, Charlie? I haven't seen you since the day before yesterday!"

"Yeah, well," Charlie said, still in his cockpit, "I'm not doing so good—I think it's my eyes—can't read the instruments anymore, and my ears—I'm having trouble with them too—can't hear the radio anymore. Don't know what I'd do if they had to talk me down some day."

"Maybe they'll just leave you up there," Bobby said, never passing up an opportunity to become part of the funny adult world.

"Oh, hi, Bobby," Charlie said, jumping from one of

the Cessna's pontoons onto the dock and snubbing a piece of rope around a post, bringing the drifting plane to an abrupt halt. "How's your father?"

"He's right here," Bobby said.

"You think so?" Charlie said.

"Are you really getting deaf and going blind?" Bobby wanted to know.

"Only when your father flies with me," Charlie said. He knew I was scared to death of planes, and he never hesitated to add to my insecurity.

Dr. Shimkin shoved the pilot's seat forward and jumped nimbly down from the plane onto the dock. He had all the spring and zip of a young man of twenty-one. As he turned, full of exuberant joy and enthusiasm, to meet Reiko and me and Bobby and Timothy, he suddenly froze as he became instantly aware that the Douglases were not alone on this tiny island in the middle of nowhere. There was a long silence where all of us seemed to be plasticized in time.

"You remember Mr. and Mrs. Harry Mitchell, Mr. and Mrs. Rogers Dotson, Mr. and Mrs. Frank Krasselt, Mr. and Mrs.—I mean, Virgil Palmquist and Reggie Mailer, from the Yellow Prune, and Bella Brown."

Dr. Shimkin looked from one face to another of the entire Honansville Ecology Group without the slightest sign of recognition. Then he turned, like an old man of eighty, and slowly started to climb back aboard the plane. He got as far as the second rung of the short ladder when a woman, who could only be described charitably as mousey-looking, appeared at the plane's only exit and started down the short ladder.

My God, I thought, they've brought their maid— where do they think they are, at the Fontainebleau?! Dr. Shimkin backed down the ladder to let the "maid" descend to the dock. Charlie Burke then reached up and hauled down two verminous-looking children, about two and four years old. Both with raw, red, runny noses, which hadn't been wiped since birth. Christ! I thought. What you have to do nowadays to keep a maid—she brings her kids along when she works.

As Charlie Burke handed down the luggage and I

159

piled it up on the dock, I kept wondering why Lillian Shimkin and her kids didn't get out of the plane, but then I thought, maybe they're penned in behind the luggage, which often happens in small planes.

"Well," Charlie said, "I guess that's about it."

"About *it?*" I said, which was hard to do with my mouth hanging so wide open.

"Yeah," Charlie said, "just call us when you want to come back out. Radio working okay?"

"Yes," I said, "working fine."

"Okay," Charlie said, unwinding the rope from the post and shoving the little Cessna out toward the center of the lake. "See you soon—unless we all get lucky. . . ." Then he turned and climbed back into his cockpit and waved as he flipped the engine switch. The prop noise echoed back and forth and up and down the lake as the plane taxied to its takeoff point.

34

AS soon as Charlie and his Cessna were disappearing over the dark trees at the far end of the lake, I turned to our "guests." The woman was standing forlornly, looking in the direction of the vanished airplane. She was dressed in dirty flared slacks and sandals, and over all this was a fringed poncho—and over the poncho was her long, disheveled hair. I presumed it was hair, although her head looked like a ripped open, seven-dollar Goodwill mattress. It didn't need a comb. It needed a good shave, so it could start over.

The two orphans, who seemed to be her children, stood off from her—forlorn on their own—trying to sniff their air passages into a somewhat better position insofar as their oxygen intake was concerned. But it was a losing battle. I felt they would be getting more air if they were *tadpoles*.

There had been deadly silence on the part of the

Honansville group all during this disembarkation sequence. Dr. Shimkin suddenly came to life, which was about the only choice he had.

"Oh," he said, to everyone lined up on the dock. "This" —indicating the ponchoed apparition—"is my—secretary. Yeah—secretary. She's gonna—she's gonna help me with my notes—notes on wolves." Dr. Shimkin managed a wan smile. "You know—typing."

Dr. Shimkin had never had a secretary before, or *any* office help. He had a reputation all over Litchfield County, Connecticut, as being a one-man show, so this suddenly announced "secretary" was greeted by silent volumes of heavy doubt.

"What about the kids?" Bella Brown wanted to know, nodding toward the two newly arrived waifs. "What are they—midget computer operators?" Virgil Palmquist sniggered at this and Reggie Mailer joined him. I couldn't really condemn them for this small rudeness, because nobody ever had a secretary who looked like what Dr. Shimkin had unearthed from some Stygian vault.

"Where's Lillian?" Alice Dotson asked, like Samuel Liebowitz might have asked someone he suspected of uxoricide. Her tone suggested that Lillian's body was now at the bottom of the Housatonic River, her pantyhose loaded with cement blocks.

"Who?" Dr. Shimkin said, putting his head right into the noose.

"Lillian," Bella Brown said, "whom we all know and love."

"Oh," Dr. Shimkin said, "Lillian—she's home with the kids."

"They always *are*," Alice Dotson said.

"Wait a minute," Dr. Shimkin said, suddenly wrenching himself together. "Lillian knows I'm up here. She knows I came up here to do research on Jack's wolves. Look!" He quickly hauled several thick note pads from his black attaché case. "Notebooks! To take notes on! And that's why I brought the two kids up here," indicating the two forlorn waifs, who were now sadly sailing bits of bark in the icy water along the edge of the airplane dock. They're Marie's kids—oh, this is Marie—

161

Marie Prindle—she had no one to leave them with while she was on this assignment—so—"

Reiko and I and the Honansville Ecology Group acknowledged this introduction, while Marie Prindle, who didn't seem too happy, tried to smile. But she couldn't quite make it, so she just exposed her obscene upper gums slightly and let it go at that.

"These your children?" I asked her. She didn't answer this, but Dr. Shimkin jumped into the void and said, "Yes, these are Marie's two little children."

The Honansville group departed in its entirety to consolidate its opinions over a few Bloody Marys, and Reiko, Bobby, Timothy, and I were left with Dr. Shimkin and his entourage.

"Are these your children?" Reiko asked Dainty Marie. Dainty Marie didn't answer, but Dr. Shimkin, anxious to avoid unpleasantries, jumped in again. "Yes, Reiko, these are Marie's two little children. Adorable things. Sherwood is two years old and Elroy is four. Elroy's the oldest."

"Remarkable," I said.

"Where's Lillian?" Reiko wanted to know, and so did I.

"Yeah," Bobby said, "and John, David, and Matthew? I wanna play with them."

"Oh," Dr. Shimkin said, "Lillian and the kids don't like the woods. They went to Fire Island—they like the ocean."

"They got an *ocean* at Fire Island?" I asked. "Does anybody *know* this?"

"Very funny, Jack," Dr. Shimkin said. Then, taking a deep, guilty breath, "Where are we going to stay? I kinda like that big cabin with the fireplace."

"Okay," I said. "And—er—er—Marie—and her—children can stay over in the caretaker's cabin."

"Yes," Reiko said. "It won't take us long to clean it up a bit." At that moment in time, somewhere in the stacked luggage, a small dog started to bark and a cat started to mew.

"What's that?" Bobby said.

"Oh, that's Marie's little dog and little cat," Dr.

162

Shimkin said. "She just couldn't leave them behind. You know how it is, Jack?"

"Well, yes," I admitted. "But up here we let *our* animals run around free, and I don't know how it's going to work out with two stranger's animals—you know, territorial imperative and all that—"

"About the caretaker's cabin, Jack," Dr. Shimkin said. "Don't bother about it. There's plenty of room for all of us in the big cabin with the fireplace—more cozy, too."

It was then it really hit me. I didn't believe the story about the "secretary" at first, but then I thought—maybe I'm wrong—research *is* tiresome at best, and if you can dictate notes instead of laboriously transcribing them yourself, it lightens the burden—not completely, but somewhat. Maybe the good doctor *did* need an amanuensis. That's what I thought until he dropped the bomb about he and Dainty Marie and the kids being more cozy—*all together* in the big cabin with the fireplace. Again I had been misled by my naïveté. But I still couldn't believe that Dr. Shimkin had planned this whole thing—that he had chosen Dainty Marie for a premeditated romp in the pine needles.

Dr. David Shimkin had the second most beautiful wife (the first being Reiko) that I had ever seen possessed by any discriminating male, and here he was dragging this gangrenous trull all the way up to Canada—and also with two children who long ago should have been adopted by the Audubon Society and placed in an aviary. I couldn't *believe* it! I couldn't believe that Dr. Shimkin, whose taste I never would question on anything —food, wines, style of dress, or women—had suddenly gone berserk and imported a monster for what appeared to be an abnormal thirst for carnal knowledge—without being directed by Mike Nichols—or influenced by Rasputin.

"I'll go make up a coupla more beds in the caretaker's cabin," Reiko said, taking things remarkably in stride. But I guess it was the only way. "Come on, Marie—you can help."

Marie, from the expression on her yellow-green-mauve face, didn't take this suggestion too kindly, but what else could she do back there in the woods, surrounded by human beings? She followed after Reiko across the little red bridge which connected our island to the mainland peninsula.

"What about Sherwood and Elroy?" I called after her.

"Oh?" she said, turning. She didn't say anything more, so I said, "Sherwood and Elroy—your *children.*"

"All children have fits," she said, reviving a line I remembered reading in *The Egg and I* back ages ago. And why Marie said it I didn't want to know.

"Go ahead, kids," Dr. Shimkin said, nudging the two little wet-nosed orphans of the impending (I felt) storm. Only then did the two follow after their ponchoed witch-mother. Bobby and Timothy tagged along, too.

"Okay, David," I said to the doctor after the group had left. "What's the story?"

"Whaddya mean, Jack?" Dr. Shimkin said. "Isn't she delightful?"

"Marie!!?"

"Yeah."

"Why did you have to haul her all the way up here?" I said. "You could have knocked her off in the back of a supermarket—on a fifty-pound sack of Idaho potatoes."

"Jack, you're being crude!"

"These are crude times," I said. "What the hell has she got under that poncho—a nymphomaniac sister?"

"She's a very nice person," Dr. Shimkin said. "I just wanted to give her and her children a few days in the country."

"You *don't* want to screw her?"

"Yes, but what's wrong with a little fresh air along with it?"

35

AFTER I had jammed Dr. Shimkin, Dainty Marie, Sherwood, and Elroy into the tiny caretaker's cabin (which was all we had available), I left for Wolf Island and the relative peace and quiet of the company of a pack of wolves. I thought, as I put-putted along in my little Springbok boat, maybe this would be what would happen to all of civilization before too long—we'd all be taking off for a Wolf Island somewhere—if there were any left, anywhere.

Wolf and Lady and Dancer, Prancer, Dunder, Blitzen, and Wolfie were very glad to see me. Because I was alone—and I was loaded with raw chicken backs.

The feeding of seven large wolves—all in one group and all very hungry, as wolves always seemed to be—was a strenuous problem. First, before I got out of the boat, I'd throw seven chicken backs in as many directions. This would scatter them, as they dashed after the choice morsels, snarling and growling hideously. This was to warn away *me* (or any of their fellows, I assumed). Maybe it was directed just against me. I had no way of knowing, never having seen a wolf pack feeding in the wild.

I was kept very busy after I left the boat with my large pail of chicken backs (and necks). I had to keep pitching like Vida Blue, but to seven different catchers—all in a very short inning. I tried to make sure that each wolf got about three or four pounds of food. This would satisfy them. In the wild, of course, they didn't always eat every day—it depended on the hunting—and they could consume enormous amounts of food. A wolf's stomach capacity is between fifteen and nineteen pounds—this is how much he will eat after the pack has killed a deer or a moose. After that, if game is scarce, he may not eat for a long time. The record for a wolf's enforced fasting is held by a Russian wolf. This animal had been wounded by hunters and remained hidden, in one spot, for seventeen days. After this he had been flushed from his hiding place and killed. He seemed, according to Russian reports, in perfect health, although very thin. Maybe the Russian reports should have put it another way—he was in perfect health until they shot him. From a plane.

After I had thrown the last chicken back I sank down exhausted against the nearest tree. The wolves, after they had satisfied themselves by sniffing all of me that I had no food left for them, formed a circle around me, seemingly in anticipation of something. I didn't know what. I was sweating despite the cold wind sweeping across the little island, and I was out of breath. All I wanted to do at the moment was lie back against the pine and rest.

As I looked around this unreal lupine circle, I saw seven magnificent creatures of the wild. Seven pairs of amber eyes stared at me. These eyes, which at one time I had thought were without expression, had softened to something resembling love. Or maybe it was gratitude at being almost free. Or maybe it wasn't. The moment was brief, but I shall never forget it. I knew then that there could be no turning back. I would soon see that they would be completely free.

Reiko had prepared a sumptuous dinner in honor of Dr. Shimkin. She served his favorite dish, something she had thought of herself. It was my favorite, too, and I don't know where she got the idea from—she had no cookbooks when we were first married and she couldn't have read them anyway. This particular specialty of Reiko's consisted of very thinly sliced corned beef cooked in some special way, with a very different sour-sweet sauce, and fried rice unlike any fried rice I had ever tasted before. I wish my readers would *write* to me about this recipe—I'm sure Reiko would want *everyone* to have it. It's so—well, it's Lucullan—that's what it is.

Reiko always makes a sensational salad, and after everyone had sat back, satiated, after two and three helpings of everything, she served strawberries and whipped cream. Even I was impressed at this—they were fresh strawberries and genuine whipped cream, from a genuine cow. How the hell did she manage this 116 miles from the nearest genuine cow? I never found out because I was too anxious to keep things running smoothly. I didn't want any unpleasantness because of Dr. Shimkin's suddenly turning into Mr. Hyde—via Danity Marie—but my fears were unfounded. Completely. After dinner Rogers Dotson accepted a brandy snifter half filled with Napoleon's favorite, then grabbed our only comfortable chair, lighted his fetid meerschaum, and got himself settled for the evening—all the while stroking his everfaithful nonexistent Irish setter.

I had built a roaring birchwood fire in the huge fireplace, and the flames threw mysterious and eerie shadows on every wall of the shiny-logged living room.

Harry Mitchell and his semilovely wife, Ruthie, had settled themselves on the polar bear rug in front of the fireplace, lolling, completely satisfied with their world and the jug of martinis which they shared with each other but no one else.

Frank and Ethel Krasselt, along with Alice Dotson, were playing Old Maid, the only card game they could find in the card game drawer of the built-in wall chest, while Bella Brown chinned herself 317 times on her portable chinning bar, which could be fitted to any convenient doorway. The convenient doorway she had chosen was the one in a passage to our only bathroom, which wasn't too convenient if one cared to wash one's hands. Bella had to be shoved to one side like drapes in order to continue one's journey toward Scottissueland. And shoving Bella to one side was like trying to open a lock in the Panama Canal by hand.

Virgil Palmquist and Reggie Mailer were busy whoopsing over photos of men's hairstyles they had found in a 1958 copy of *Esquire*.

No one was paying the slightest attention to Dr. Shimkin, who was paying more than adequate attention to his "secretary." He was catering to her every wish and command, which was difficult to do because Dainty Marie was ignoring him completely.

She was also ignoring the wailings of her progeny, Sherwood and Elroy, who demanded, besides attention: Cokes, cookies, candy, jello, ice cream, and cigarettes. And right *now!*

Reiko gave each of them a bag of marshmallows and told them to play with Bobby and Timothy. The marshmallows and the suggestion did not quiet them. They got louder. It was then that Dainty Marie volunteered the charming information that her children both had mosquito bites which apparently had become infected and would not heal.

"Looks like you shoulda brought your little black bag with you," I said to Dr. Shimkin.

Dr. Shinkin said to me, "I did." Then to Dainty Marie, "Let's see those mosquito bites, My Dear." Dainty Marie started to take off her clothes.

"No, no, no," Dr. Shimkin said. "The *kids'* mosquito bites!"

"I have 'em, too," Dainty Marie said.

"Later. *Later,*" Dr. Shimkin said, with a suggestion of leer.

After Sherwood and Elroy were stripped, Dr. Shimkin examined them from stem to stern—mostly stern, because that's where the main trouble seemed to be.

"Hmmmmmmmmm," Dr. Shimkin hmmmmmmmmed, about eight times. So I took a look. It wasn't too pleasant. Whatever these kids had, it wasn't mosquito bites. To me it looked like yaws. I don't know exactly what yaws is, but the natives of Africa and the South Pacific get them all the time. And what these kids had looked like "yaws" sounds.

"What is it, Doctor?" I said. "Yaws?"

"Hmmmmmmmm," Dr. Shimkin insisted for a total of thirteen times in all.

"Look," Dainty Marie said, "they're mosquito bites— they got 'em last August. They'll be all right. All kids get mosquito bites."

"Since August they've been this way?" I asked.

"What's on television?" Dainty Marie wanted to know, hurriedly slapping the kids' wardrobe back on them, which didn't take long because they hadn't been allowed to hear about underwear, as yet.

"Hmmmmmmm," Dr. Shimkin said.

"I'll turn the set on," I said, and I did. But the set did not light up or hum or flip the pictures around or pull sideways. It didn't do anything. I tried to light an electric light (the power coming from one of our two Kohler generators). The light didn't light.

"It's the generator," Reiko said, womanlike, predicting the worst. But she was right. It was the generator— or I should say it was both generators. Neither worked, which was odd because they both had worked perfectly for more than five years.

"You got candles?" Dr. Shimkin asked.

"Yes," Reiko said, "we've got plenty of candles." Which I was surprised to hear.

"We've got plenty of flashlights, too," Reiko said.

"Good."

"But the batteries all have green stuff leaking out of them." That left us with just candles, which was all right. They made plenty of light for Sherwood and Elroy to see what bric-a-brac they were breaking but not enough illumination for the adults who spent most of the evening, when they got up to go to the bar, tripping over half-full Coke bottles abandoned on the floor by Sherwood and Elroy after a couple of sips. The air traffic in loud "goddammits!" was a little heavier than usual.

Life seemed strange without an evening of television, but it took on a new meaning with the never-ending mullygutsing of Sherwood and Elroy and the continuously yapping toy mutt, which Dainty Marie never traveled without. An interval of amateau first-aid practice was added when Dainty Marie's sneaky, cockeyed Siamese cat swiped a long claw mark on Timothy's cheek when he tried to hug it. It wasn't a very deep scratch, and it didn't bleed much, but Reiko was all for applying a tourniquet (very hard to apply with a face wound) and giving him a shot of something to ease the pain, which Timothy hadn't noticed until Reiko called his attention to it. Then he screamed with the unfairness of it all. And it was unfair—his 200-pound mountain lion had never so much as bruised him, and now he had been done in by

169

a scraggly, treacherous, 3-pound cockeyed cat. We took his wooden samurai sword away from him just in time.

When I had the temerity to suggest to Dainty Marie that, so far as I could ascertain, neither animal was housebroken, she replied somewhat heatedly that that was the trouble with America—everyone should be allowed to do their thing. And that's exactly the way it worked out. The little mutt, straining so hard I thought he would wind up inverted, finally did his thing in the center of the living-room floor, and the cat urinated into the floor furnace vent, making the atmosphere in the room smell more lemonier than ever.

Cats must have a thing for floor vents, because Pussycat, our mountain lion, did it all the time, which, when you think of it, does make for dispatch and neatness.

Without television the rest of our candlelit evening was spent with an almost reverential quiet. None of us had ever experienced such a pleasant evening—somehow we didn't realize yet that we were not being entertained. We were entertaining ourselves. Unheard of in living mmory.

36

THE morning after our televisionless night was cold. Cold and gloomy. The sky was a darkening gray. Foreboding. The pines, cedars, and hemlocks bordering Lost Lake were black. The waters of the lake were black. My coffee was as black as my mood, because I didn't like my coffee black. But there was no cream—and no nondairy substitute, either.

"Why don't you call Canada Goose and ask them to bring up some cream?" Reiko suggested. It was almost her *last* suggestion.

"Pay sixty dollars air fare to bring cream?!" I said, marveling at my self-control.

"That's a lot of money for cream, Mommie," Bobby said.

"Money for cream," Timothy parroted.

"I meant—if Charlie Burke or any of the others are coming up this way, they can drop it off," Reiko said, which actually made sense, because bush pilots are the most accommodating people on earth—nothing is too much trouble, and even if they have nothing to deliver—such as the mail, or cream—they'll touch down on our remote lake just to see if everything is okay.

"I'll give 'em a call and see if anybody is coming up this way," I said, walking to the radio, which is located behind the bar. I turned it on and waited the minute or so it takes to warm up. It didn't warm up. It didn't sparkle with static, as it does quite often. It didn't do anything. I turned the volume up to full blast and yelled louder than I had meant into the mouthpiece, "VXZ69 calling Chinookville!—VXZ69 calling Chinookville!" I kept this up. Over and over again—my desperation building rapidly as no reassuring "This is Chinookville —go ahead" came from the speaker. After five minutes of this, Dr. Shimkin, who on that dark day looked more like the patient instead of the doctor, managed to say to Reiko as he entered the living room, "What's the cubmaster up to?"

"He's trying to call the Canada Goose Airways, but nobody answers," Reiko said.

"Oh," Dr. Shimkin said. Then with difficulty, he had a thought. "Anything wrong?"

"Yes," Reiko said. Then as she didn't volunteer what, Dr. Shimkin had to ask, "What?"

"We're all out of cream. I forgot to buy it," Reiko said. "Jack wants it for his coffee."

"Oh," Dr. Shimkin said, and threw himself into *my* easy chair, while I continued with my "VXZ69 calling Chinookville!"

"Why doesn't Jack use milk? Practically the same," Dr. Shimkin said.

"We don't have any milk," Reiko said.

The doctor straightened up like a shot. "No milk? What do Bobby and Timothy drink?"

"Bobby drinks apple juice and Timothy drinks ginger ale. They don't like milk."

171

"What about Sherwood and Elroy? What the hell are *they* gonna drink? You got any powdered milk?"

"No," Reiko said. "I threw it out. Every time I gave it to Bobby and Timothy it made them sneeze."

"You're supposed to mix it with *water!*" Dr. Shimkin said, not trying very hard to remain unexasperated.

I gave up trying to raise Chinookville and Canada Goose Airways on the radio. "Goddamn radio isn't working," I informed an already informed gathering.

"How about the generator?" Dr. Shimkin asked.

"Oh, my God!" I said. "That's right—how could the radio work if the generator isn't—generating! Why the hell didn't we bring along a battery set? Then we wouldn't have to depend on that goddamn generator!"

"You got a book on generators?" Dr. Shimkin said.

"I have a *library* on generators!" I said. This was all too true. I must have at least twenty-four volumes on the inner working and history of the generator, from 1912 up to the present day, plus a trunk full of clippings from *Popular Mechanics* and *Unpopular Mechanics* explaining as gently as possible that the best thing for you to do would be to leave the whole thing up to a generator repairman. Nevertheless, whenever anything goes awry, I alway reach for my well-nigh immaculate *Generator Repairing for the Beginner* and read the first paragraph on page one: "A—Remove the trunnion and gudgeon; B—unscrew the servomotor plate and examine the transducer manostat—it may be malfunctioning; C—" I never get to "C." By that time *I'm* malfunctioning—because of my appalling ignorance of a simple gadget like a transducer manostat.

"Well, we'll look at the generator after breakfast," Dr. Shimkin said. "We gotta call that bush pilot because I gotta leave."

"You just got here," Reiko said, as she steamed up a barrel of rice on our enormous lumberjack-type camp stove.

"I know," Dr. Shimkin said, clamping a black-ribboned gold-rimmed pince-nez to the bridge of his nose, "but I'm a dedicated man. I mustn't forget my Hippocratic Oath. I have my patients to think about."

172

"Your Hippocratic Oath starts out with, 'Our Father who art in heaven—' " I said.

"Only if I get a chance to treat *you,*" he said.

"What's the matter, Doc?" I said. "Didn't things work out last night?"

"I beg your pardon?"

"With you and Miss Planet of the Apes?"

"I gotta get out of here—I gotta get away from those kids—they didn't sleep all night long."

"No romance, huh?"

"Are you kidding?! It would have been like doing it between halves on the fifty-yard line in the Rose Bowl."

"Well," I said, "if we can't fix the generator, you'd better get used to the idea of having an audience if you can't control your beastly instincts, because we have no way of contacting anyone to get you—or us—out of here. Unless you want to walk."

"How far?" Dr. Shimkin wanted to know, getting up and flexing his leg muscles.

"Well," I said, "if you just go as far as our mailbox it'll take you three days."

"What?" he said, dropping all of his flexed muscles dejectedly into a chair.

"It doesn't seem like much when you're flying in here," I said, "but walking in is really tough—or walking out. You've got swamps, tree stumps, big rocks—mosquitoes, deer flies—you might even meet a disagreeable bear. But, then again," I continued, rubbing it in a bit, "maybe after a few days more with that little mother you brought up here—a bear might not look too bad." The doctor groaned.

Dainty Marie and Sherwood and Elroy opened the front door and came in. The doctor didn't jump to his feet and click his heels as he had done periodically and incessantly the night before. He just sat and stared at his apparently newly discovered fingernails. He checked both hands, and sure enough he had four or five on each hand.

"Breakfast ready?" Dainty Marie wanted to know. in what could only be described as a very snotty tone. Even Reiko, whose soft answers (when she is in the

173

mood) hath turned away much wrath, was nettled by this imperious question.

"No, it isn't," she said, "but it's almost time for lunch."

"My kids gotta eat right now!" Dainty Marie said.

"I think I'll go for the mail," Dr. Shimkin said, heading for the door. "See you in a week." I knew he wasn't silly enough to try for the big one so I didn't answer.

"We have no milk," Reiko said. "I'm sorry."

"How about Coke?" Dainty Marie asked.

"You mean the kids have Coke for breakfast?" I said.

"What's wrong with Coke?" she wanted to know. Reiko gave Sherwood and Elroy each a bottle of Coke. Elroy promptly dropped his on the floor, and after waiting a moment for Dainty Marie to mop up the mess, Reiko picked up the now emptied bottle and spread a few newspapers to stop up the liquid.

I explained, "The New York *Times*—it's the quicker picker upper."

Dainty Marie didn't react to this more-or-less bon mot. She just sat down in the chair recently vacated by Dr. Shimkin and said, "Where's the morning paper?"

"We don't have the morning paper," I said.

"How about last night's?" she said.

"We don't even have last *year's*," I said. This set the tone for the day. Dainty Marie spent most of it smoking three or four packs of cigarettes and drinking a gallon and a half of black coffee. She looked, after a while, like an ugly cobra that had just been drummed out of a Cambodian snake temple and was in the mood for nothing.

Sherwood and Elroy were fed and cared for by Reiko, who didn't particularly like anybody else's kids—as who did--but she couldn't let them live on Cokes alone. She shoved the rice down them like she was fattening them for a Japanese Thanksgiving.

Dr. Shimkin and I worked on and over and under the generators, but we never did find the transducer manostat—or anything else mentioned in the manual or the generator library. I finally guessed that we had fed it a bad batch of gasoline, which was the fuel it used.

174

This one particular drum had been sitting in our storage bin for a year, and that's not good for gasoline—it gets gummy, which could screw up the best of generators. By hand cranking we got one of them to operate a few minutes at a time, and I would run the 220-yard dash to the radio and scream out, "VXZ69 calling Chinookville!" about forty times, but I'm sure the signal hadn't traveled more than a sixteenth of a mile—if that—from our transmitter. After a long, hopeless day we had to admit it—we were marooned in the deep, deep, DEEP woods, and our supply of Cokes was dangerously low. We were on the verge of being in trouble.

37

A WEEK had passed, and there was very little our *guests* and our *family* had left—in *common*. The generator would no longer crank, and we had long ago given up on trying to communicate with the outside world. Or each other. After we knew the generators had gone to that big Westinghouse in the sky, we tried smoke signals—a futile task, as there was no one to receive them out there in the great beyond. Even the smoke signals were a flop. I had always understood that oil, when burned in the open, would fulminate great gouts of black smoke. Don't you believe it! Those oil rig fires you see burning in the Gulf of Mexico are a canard. The television cameramen flying around in helicopters use special lenses to darken the smoke so you'll get a better picture on your set. This *must* be it—*we* filled a tin drum half full of oil and set it afire—and got the purest, thinnest, whitest smoke I have ever imagined. It couldn't have been seen more than fifteen feet away. This nonexistent signal fire smoke was what we had counted on to arouse the curiosity of an Ontario Lands and Forests fire-spotting plane and spur it to fly over and investigate—then we would immediately take one of our outboard motorboats to the center of the lake and circle in a very tight circle and at a fairly fast speed. This was the signal of distress, according to my *How to Survive in the Woods* book. This, of course, was the distress sign in the summer. The book doesn't mention what you do on the ground in the *winter* in order to alert a plane that you are in trouble. Maybe they figure that in the winter you're not going to survive any-way—and some winters they could be right.

The oil fire we had created burned for days, because we hadn't the slightest idea of how to extinguish it, and so it shouldn't be a *total* waste we had outdoor barbecues on it.The hamburgers and hotdogs had a distinctive Good Gulf flavor, but they were better than all-bran to keep you right on schedule.

Finally, after the eighth day, Reiko announced, "We have no more hamburger and we have no more hot dogs."

"What have we got?" I asked.

"Chicken backs," Reiko said.

"Oh, no!" I said, very definitely. "The chicken backs are for the wolves—they come first—that's why we're here."

"You mean," Reiko said, "the wolves come first before Harry and Ruthie Mitchell, Frank and Ethel Krasselt, Rogers and Alice Dotson, Bella Brown, Virgil Palmquist, Reggie Mailer, Dr. Shimkin and that girl, and Sherwood and Elroy, and Bobby, Timothy, and me?"

"Yes."

Reiko was shocked. This confirmed it. I liked animals better than my family. This wasn't true, but I was de-termined to protect my plentiful supply of chicken backs, which I had secreted in large, thin wooden crates, just as they had come from Mr. Perdue, in our ice house. They were buried deep under huge chunks of ice and tons of sawdust. It also wasn't true that I was going to withhold the wolves' chicken backs if they could keep Reiko, Bobby, and Timothy from starving. When I told Reiko this, tears welled up in her beautiful brown eyes. She hadn't married Count Dracula after all. She put her arms around me, and so did Bobby. Then Timothy put his tiny arms around Bobby, and that started a fight.

Bobby didn't want any affection from his little brother. We didn't have a sibling rivalry problem in our little group—we had World War III—every other day. And twice on Sundays.

"What about our guests?" Reiko asked, breaking away back to her rice pot. "There may be trouble if they get hungry enough to eat chicken backs—and you won't give them any."

"If they get that hungry," I said, "I'll show 'em one —and if that doesn't discourage them, I'll feed them all at Wolf Island—at the same time I feed the wolves."

"You gonna take movies of that, Papa?" Bobby wanted to know.

"Good idea, Bobby," I said. "I'll show 'em on the Johnny Carson show."

"Better for *Laugh-In*," Bobby suggested.

Dainty Marie and Sherwood and Elroy materialized from nowhere. None of them ever made a sound when they came or left.

"Lunch ready?" Dainty Marie said, now even more insolent and contemptuous than she had appeared when she and her two fungus-children first arrived at Lost Lake.

"You like chicken backs?" Bobby asked her warily. She looked at him with her heavy-lidded cobra eyes and said nothing.

"It's wolf food," Bobby said, expecting a reaction which never came.

"We don't *have* any chicken backs!" I proclaimed loudly to the world, "but we do have quite a few extra cans of Alpo." I said this last hovering over Dainty Marie like a solicitous but unshaven head waiter at the best French restaurant in town with a large clientele of Park Avenue dogs.

Dainty Marie ignored me completely. She sat down on the floor in front of the fireplace, drew her begrimed poncho closer around her, and lit a cigarette. She had lost interest in food, and she seemed to have lost any regard, if she ever had any, for the two victims of motherhood—her children.

I was beginning to feel very sorry for Sherwood and

Elroy and as unflattering as I have pictured them, I felt they deserved *some* love and attention. From *someone*. They didn't *ask* to be born—or, if they did, this should teach them a lesson to never speak to strangers. The stranger was Dainty Marie—a Madonna without portfolio.

I had never seen or heard either Sherwood or Elroy laugh—or maybe it was because no one tried to make them.

"You know what I'm gonna do?" I said to them. "Later on, maybe tonight, I'm gonna be the Easter Bunny for you two—and I'm gonna go *alllllll* over the living room and lay eggs—colored eggs. Would you like that?"

There was not the slightest flicker from either Sherwood or Elroy that I had even been speaking to them but Bobby said, "How you gonna lay eggs, Papa? We don't have any eggs left."

"The *Easter Bunny's* got *plenty* of *eggs!*" I said, giving Bobby the cold eye.

"I wish the Easter Bunny laid hamburgers instead of eggs," Bobby said.

"For Chrissake, Bobby," I said. "I'm trying to bring a little *sunshine* into these kids' lives and you keep interrupting!"

Bobby pouted, and suddenly both Sherwood and Elroy started to sing, "You are my sunshine—my only sunshine—" in a glazed, somber monotone. They sounded like two dead Lennon Sisters.

"My God!" Bobby said. "They're *singing!*"

"Yeah," I said, "and all this time I thought they were *dancers.*" This was lost on Bobby, and I was saved from explaining by Dr. Shimkin's entrance.

It was lunchtime, and Dr. Shimkin said he was very hungry. He decided against Alpo.

"It's not horsemeat, Doc," I said, knowing his passion for horses. "It's beef and beef by-products."

"What *by*-products?"

"It doesn't say, but there must be an awful lot of odds and ends in a cow that we don't know about that are perfectly edible," I said.

"People are perfectly edible," Dr. Shimkin said, "but how many of us take advantage of that fact?"

"Well," I said, "the Donner party, for a starter."

"That was different," Dr. Shimkin said. "They were caught in the high Sierra snow and they were starving."

"Papa," Bobby said, "it's starting to snow a little bit."

"I'll toss you for Elroy," I said to the good doctor.

"What about Sherwood?" he said.

"The *wolves* gotta *eat*, too."

"That's an idea," I said.

"Gee, Papa," Bobby said, "would you feed Sherwood to the *wolves?*"

"Would *you* wanna eat him?" I asked Bobby. Bobby ran from the room, gagging.

By this time Reiko had had enough of this "funny talk," as she put it. "We have enough food for a while," she said. "We have peanut butter, rice, potato chips, flour, maple syrup, sugar, coffee, and about five pounds of M & M's."

"You mean—look, Ma, no chocolate on hands? Those M & M's?"

"Yes."

"Five pounds," I said, "to be divided equally among seventeen starving people."

"Papa!" Bobby came rushing back into the house. "Papa, I hear a plane!"

Reiko, Dr. Shimkin, Bobby, Timothy, Sherwood, and Elroy were outside in a flash. The Cobra Lady was now cast in bronze—she didn't even move her eyes. The plane was miles and miles away just disappearing over the horizon. Our invisible burning oil invited not even a *dipping* of *wings!*

"Goddamn sonsabitches!" I said, unreasonably. "What the hell ever happened to all those goddamn planes that used to drop in and see if we were okay, or dropped down here to go fishing? Or those sonofabitchin' hunters who used to shoot up the whole place trying to get a moose? Or even just some bastard who's lost—he could take a message out to Chinookville."

"If he was lost, how could he ever find Chinookville?"

179

Reiko said. I ignored this and resolved to devote the afternoon to getting schlocked.

"Papa," Bobby said, "why don't we write a message on a piece of paper and put it in a bottle and throw it in the lake—maybe somebody will find it and come and rescue us."

"An excellent suggestion!" Dr. Shimkin said.

"Yeah," I said, less than tenderly, "maybe some beaver who can read will find it and tell Dear Abby—then we won't have anything to worry about except Dear Abby." I resolved to devote the *rest* of my *life* to getting schlocked and smoking marijuana in a nose pipe—with a mixture of snuff and bear grease (in case my sinuses became too arid).

"You're bitter, Papa," Bobby said. I knew the kid was right, but I had about had it with unneeded guests. And you don't realize how *un*-needed guests can be until you know they *aren't* going to *leave! Ever!*

38

I HAD done everything I could to avoid personality clashes with the Honansville Ecology Group, which was rapidly losing interest in Mother Nature.

"What I wouldn't give," Harry Mitchell said, after a particularly trying day of forcing themselves to be really interested in the flora and fauna of the great North Chinook Bay Wilderness Reserve, in which they were now stranded, "for a good look at the good old Housatonic River in good old Connecticut. I'd even like to take a drink from it."

"That's all you'd have to do," I reminded him, "and you'd have immediate and terminal diarrhea."

"I don't care," Harry Mitchell said. "I'm goddamn sick of all this goddamn fresh air and the goddamn clean skies and the goddamn pure water!"

"Don't forget the goddamn peace and quiet," I said.

180

"Yeah," Harry Mitchell agreed. "I'd love to hear a great big eighty-ton gravel truck go barreling down the road in front of my house—and a few screaming motorcycles going by at midnight. This goddamn silence up in this goddamn God-forsaken country—I'm *hearing* things!"

This was from not only Harry Mitchell. And his semi-lovely wife, Ruthie. The whole "Group" was beginning to feel this way. Rogers Dotson had run out of fuel for his stinking pipe at the same time discovering that there was no faithful Irish setter under his everstroking hand. The combination of these two cataclysmic incidences unhinged him a bit and he wandered around through the blueberry bushes on our little island mumbling somethimg about McDonald's and "Big Mac"— whoever *he* was.

Virgil Palmquist and Reggie Mailer, who were so entranced with the great age of the enormous trees surrounding Lost Lake, now never wanted to see anything old again. When—and if—they got back to Honansville they were going to sell their antique shop and buy a Saab agency where there was no such thing as an old used car. "A Saab lasts forever in Sweden," Reggie said.

"Not quite," Virgil disagreed, "but when a Saab dies in Sweden they give it a Viking funeral—you know, flaming torches—then they all put on those horny hats and at the grave they have a ball."

"Sweden sounds like fun," Reggie said. "Why don't we go there?"

"I'd like to if we ever get out of here," Virgil said. "How the hell did we ever get mixed up in the ecology bag anyway?!"

"It was *your* idea," Reggie said.

"It was not—now that I remember. It was *yours!*" Virgil said.

"You're mad! Absolutely mad!" Reggie said.

"Really?" Virgil said and slapped Reggie. Then Reggie slapped Virgil, and for three days afterward they both nursed pursed lips.

Frank and Ethel Krasselt and Alice Dotson played

181

Old Maid for hours and hours and hours. They had long forgotten what game it was they were playing and they also failed to notice that half the Old Maid deck was now old baseball cards, which had somehow in their numbness become mixed in. Not that it mattered. They were also betting heavily. As of that morning, Alice Dotson owed Frank and Ethel Krasselt fourteen million, three hundred and eighty seven dollars. This game kept them occupied and quiet until Frank and Ethel refused to extend Alice any more credit.

Bella Brown took the whole thing in stride. Literally. She had walked all around the lake seven times in seven days. Every morning she crashed off through the bush and crashed back at dusk. Poor Bella, she didn't realize what she was doing to the ecology of our area. We hadn't seen a moose drinking from the lake for a week.

I had two methods of defense against this mass "cabin fever." I had my painting and my wolves. My painting had nothing to do with art. It had to do with maintenance. The previous owner of our camp must have at one time attended a sale of red paint, because we had enough red paint stored in the boathouse to last for the next seventy years—even if we were careless.

I started painting the roof of every cabin, and there were thirteen in all, red. Every day, all day, I painted roofs—red. Finally, because I had misjudged, I *finished* painting all the roofs—red. From the air it must have looked like Canada had been wounded. If anyone had ever flown over to see it.

Also every day, Dr. Shimkin and I boated over to Wolf Island, where I fed the wolves and he took notes. He rapidly filled hundreds of pages with tightly written notes. He said instead of a paper on wolves to be read at the Las Vegas AMA convention he was going to do a *book* on wolves. As he had already written a smashingly best-selling book on sex, which everyone in America bought, this was probably his atonement.

Not that anything could atone for all the damage that a good sex manual could do to a successful marriage.

Dr. Shimkin pointed out all the obvious things about

182

my seven wolves which I had not really noticed. He made me aware of the other facial expressions of the wolf in relation to its inner workings—the activity of the eyes, the nose, and the ears all meant something—something a little more subtle than I had noticed. It was no trick to be very aware of a wolf with teeth bared, lips rolled back and the ears pulled forward, and the eyes seemingly shooting sparks. Any dolt would recognize these things as fraught with unsocial indications, but there were other things too: A wolf with his tail almost straight up as he stands or walks means that he has self-confidence and usually would be a dominant wolf. A slight crook in the tail when raised means a certain threat—to another wolf—either at feeding time or when a wolf doesn't feel up to a game or any social intercourse. A wolf tail hung straight down, with a slight curl, can mean a not-entire threat, but it behooves any other wolf approaching this animal to use some care.

Of course, the submissive animals always carry their tails low, or between their legs, which is not so different from dogs.

There were many other things Dr. Shimkin spotted immediately, due to his youthful experience of his year's study of the wolves of Canada's vast Northwest Territories. He was the naturalist and could be dispassionate about these animals. I was the wolf lover, and I really didn't notice or care too much about their tail positions. I just wanted them to be wolves—and healthy—and happy.

One day while Dr. Shimkin was there on Wolf Island we tried a couple of weird experiments to help them get the idea of hunting for themselves. The doctor had brought up several stuffed rabbits, which were to be hurled about, and the wolves were to chase these stuffed skins and somehow get the idea that that's what was expected of them in the wild. It didn't work out that way at all. The doctor brought his rabbits ashore on the island as the wolves came down to meet us. He expected they would all start jumping up and ripping the stuffed bunnies from his arms, but nothing like that happened. Even when he pitched them with all his force across the open spot at the boat landing, Wolf, Lady, and their five pups were only mildly interested. They sauntered over and sniffed the fakes, then sauntered back.

"What the hell's the matter?" Dr. Shimkin said. "Don't they wanna *chase* anything?"

"I guess they've caught too many wild rabbits on the island here," I said, "to be interested in stuffed ones."

"Oh," Dr. Shimkin said, rather annoyed because he had carried these full dozen stuffed bunnies in his arms all the way from Honansville. His fellow passengers on the Air Canada plane to Chinookville thought he was some kind of *weird* fur fetishist.

With the second strange experiment we tried we had a little more success, but the result was not conclusive. We had on the living-room floor of the main lodge a large, very heavy, very moth-eaten and worn polar bear rug. The head, which had been stuffed with some kind of extra-heavy cement, had its mouth open, and its mouth was full of wicked-looking yellowed teeth. The idea we had in mind was to find out whether Wolf, Lady, and Dancer, Prancer, Dunder, Blitzen, and Wolfie would attack an animal larger than a rabbit or a squirrel. Dr. Shimkin, I, and the ancient polar bear skin were to be the larger animal. Theoretically, the idea would appear sound—to a mongoloid idiot. In practice we had some difficulty.

First, after feeding them, Dr. Shimkin and I had to disembark from Wolf Island, leaving the seven wolves staring mournfully after us as we boated to a nearby very small island to get changed.

After what seemed like an impossible struggle, because the empty polar bear skin was enormously heavy, we got the thing over us. Then I, being the rear end of the polar bear, had to start the boat motor again and head back to Wolf Island, steering almost by instinct and a small hole.

"Jesus Christ, this thing is heavy!" Dr. Shimkin said. "And hot!"

"It has to be," I said. "Polar bears don't come from

184

Miami Beach. They need all the heat they can get."

"Well, they got it," he said.

By this time we had bumped the rock we used as a landing on Wolf Island—a little harder than I intended —and the polar bear collapsed as we both were sent sprawling to the wet floor of the boat.

"Jesus!" I said loudly, as I tried to massage my shins back to life.

"Shhhhhhhh!" Dr. Shimkin said. "We're not supposed to be a talking bear—we're supposed to be an eating bear."

"Okay," I said. "Let's go. I just hope they don't bite too deep."

The whole nutty project was doomed from the first, I thought, but Dr. Shimkin seemed quite pleased. The wolves, all seven of them, after acting very spooky and suspicious at first, suddenly hit us from all sides, and in nothing flat they had the polar bear rug off us and on-to the forest floor. A few moments later it was shredded.

"Aha—you see," Dr. Shimkin said happily. "That's why they ignored the stuffed bunnies—they were waiting for a stuffed polar bear!"

I didn't hold with this theory at all, because I felt that with all of Dr. Shimkin's scientific knowledge of wolves, I knew some of their traits a lot better than he. Wolf, Lady, and the five pups would have stripped us of our outer covering just as quickly if we had been wearing an old army blanket. The wolves, as all wolves, enjoyed a jolly good game of fun. I didn't think we proved a thing, and I told Dr. Shimkin this.

"That's where you're wrong, My Boy," he said. He always called me My Boy when he was annoyed with my "crackpot" theories.

"I hope you're right," I said. "I hope they're ready for bigger game, because it's getting near the time when they won't have any choice."

"Don't worry about them," Dr. Shimkin said. But I did worry—the way a mother worries every first time she sends her child to nursery school—to kindergarten —to elementary school—to day camp—to the draft board.

39

DURING the long boat ride back to "Andersonville," as I now called our unhappy camp, Dr. Shimkin reverted from the carefree anthropologist playing with wolves to a *Weltschmerz*ian zombie, fingering the handle of his eight-inch bowie knife. which he wore as part of his woodsman's outfit. He gripped the handle a few times and withdrew the wicked blade an inch or two from its leather sheath.

"If you're going to cut your throat, Doctor," I said, "would you mind doing it on the shore? I'm damn sick and tired of bailing this boat."

"Why should I cut my throat?" Dr. Shimkin said. "I've got everything to live for."

"You mean you finally made it with Dainty Marie?" I asked. which is something I've never done before in my life—questioned another man about his sex life. They usually tell you about it before you can ask.

"Ha!" Dr. Shimkin snorted at my silly question. Evidently he had *not* made it with Dainty Marie, and he was suffering. Dainty Marie now. after more than a week of Dr. Shimkin's nugatory erections. represented to him a combination of Raquel Welch. Ursula Andress, and Elizabeth Taylor all packaged into one big tunnel of love—which was closed for the winter.

As I steered the small boat through the ice-chunked water toward our home island. Dr. Shimkin looked haggard. The failing light of the late October day made the shadows of his hollowed cheeks deeper. He looked gaunt. He was unspent, and when he thought of Dainty Marie's untapped (by him) treasure, the copper buttons of his Levis would pop. Which was not the fault of the manufacturer—I'm sure Mr. Levi never intended his Levis to adequately contain a perpetual, throbbing, Jewish Tower of Pisa.

I wanted to ease Dr. Shimkin's pang of unrequited passion, so after a while I said, grasping at straws, as it were, "Doctor, have you ever thought about necrophilism?"

"You mean—as a hobby?" Dr. Shimkin said, not quite believing what he had heard. I continued this bizarre line, like a demented psychiatrist.

"No, as a solution," I said. "Why don't you take Dainty Marie out in a boat—fishing—then when you get around the point, where I don't have to be a witness, do a Dreiser."

"You mean *drown* Dainty Marie?" Dr. Shimkin said. He was really alert now.

"Yes," I said. "Didn't you study Dreiser in medical school?"

"The medical school I went to," Dr. Shimkin said gloomily, "didn't say *anything* about him."

"Strange."

"They didn't even mention Band-Aids—or aspirin."

"Christ!" I said. "Those are the two most important words in the English language!"

"I know," Dr. Shimkin said, "but when you're having trouble learning the difference between the uvula and the uterus you don't make waves. You keep your mouth shut."

"Yeah," I said. Then veering back to our original subject, "How about it—are you gonna drown Marie?"

"I don't think so," Dr. Shimkin said.

"Just trying to be helpful," I said. "She wouldn't have any choice then—you could do what you wanted."

"My God," Dr. Shimkin said, "you *are* a Martian!"

40

AT the beginning of our thirteenth day of isolation at Lost Lake, our little portable radio went dead —right after the local early morning announcer's words, "We're having technical difficulties with *God's Word for Today*—" And then nothing. Silence. Deadly silence.

Rogers Dotson took his long-cold meerschaum out of his discouraged mouth and said, "Goddamn cheap Japanese radios!"

"This cheap Japanese radio," I said, "was manufactured in Camden, New Jersey."

"Horrible state, New Jersey," Rogers Dotson continued. "Run by the Mafia."

"What about Princeton?" Virgil Palmquist wanted to know. "That's in New Jersey."

"Run by the Mafia," Rogers Dotson said and went back to his silent pipe-sucking and his five-year-old New York *Times*.

"What a peculiar old man," Reggie Mailer said.

"*I* always thought so," Alice Dotson agreed.

"I wonder what happened to *God's Word for Today?*" said Bella Brown, who for all her brawn and bravado was filled with more than a modicum of spirituality, plus less than a modicum of voodooism. But not too much less.

I was wondering too about the strange termination of our only contact with civilization. It sounded final— like maybe even God had no more words for us. I didn't mean just us stranded at Lost Lake. I meant *all* of us. All *over*.

Almost immediately I missed the radio because it was my only reassurance that there *was* a *world* out there. *Somewhere*. I could no longer hear the voice of the local incessantly overstimulated disc jockey, with all his excessive "now" verbiage, which was not only annoying—it was passé. He used phrases that had gone out of style back in the summer of '72. But as the day changed from dawn to noon to afternoon to evening, I missed him. I missed him very much. How did I know *what* was going on out there now? Maybe great events were taking place of which I, in my backwoods isolation, was not aware. Maybe the Chinese had sent more than a *delegation* to the United Nations—maybe they'd sent a couple of divisions. For all *we* knew Kissinger might be out—and Archie Bunker might be in.

Or maybe there was *nothing* out there. Maybe Ghana had had the bomb all the time and mailed it to all the other countries in the world (Special Handling) and sometime during our radio blackout had pressed a button and pow! Ghana was now number one, and our new rulers were Dick Kenyatta and Spiro Mombassa. I murmured a small prayer of thanks that I had never had a cross word with *any* Ghanamanian. I don't know why I worried about this—if *we* were the only *non-blacks* left we wouldn't be *enemies* anymore—we'd be *celebrities*. Then, again, I could be wrong about this.

In all my preparations during my lifetime to be ready for any eventuality, I tried to be more or less capable of, if not being able to completely turn aside any catastrophe, blunting the edge of adversity so it wouldn't cut quite so deeply; but in this particular calamitous situation of the total obliteration of a disc jockey, I had no weapon at my command with which to fight off the sudden silence. A silence which, in the deep, dark, and now foreboding forest, *screamed!*

I wanted to run outside and scream back, but I *couldn't. I* was the *leader!* I couldn't show any sign of weakness. I couldn't give way. I had to be strong, like Ranger Rick, who was, in a monthly magazine Bobby received, a gutsy raccoon, who wore a Boy Scout hat, and gave out with homely little words of encouragement to all the little folk who lived in the forest. Like us.

The evening of the fourteenth day of our exile almost changed my whole life. I was offered a chance for instant leprosy. Dainty Marie made a pass at me. I guess that's what silence does to some people.

"A penny for your thoughts?" Dainty Marie said to me and grabbed my surprised crotch with a skilled talon as I stood in the dark, looking out across the Stygian waters of Lost Lake. Before we were marooned, they were velvety black—now they were Stygian.

"What?" I said, nonplussed.

"I said, 'A penny for your thoughts,'" she said, at the same time maneuvering a firmer hold on all that I held dear. I felt like I was being groped by an iron claw machine.

"Be careful," I said. "My chinos have been blessed by the archbishop."

"Nuts!" she said.

"And rinsed in holy water," I said, not knowing whether she was speaking anatomically or derisively.

"Do you or don't you?" Dainty Marie said, with a tug which traveled all the way up to the top of my head in the form of a hot meteor which exploded just in back of my cerebrum. At this point I prayed that everything was still attached.

"Look," I said breathlessly, which she misunderstood, "you're Doc Shimkin's girl——"

"Fuck him!" she said.

"Well—yes," I agreed. "That was the whole point of this trip."

"I wouldn't touch him if he had a ten-foot pole," she said. I think that's what she said.

"Look," I said, "I'm very flattered by your kind offer, but I just couldn't. I'm one of those dopes that's in love with his wife."

"What's love got to do with it?"

"Well—"

"I mean—look—we're stuck way up here in this strung-out country—no television—no radio—no hamburgers—what the hell else is there to do?"

"I never thought of it quite that way," I said, which was a big fat lie.

"Well, *think* about it," Dainty Marie said, moving her writhing stomach closer to my nervous one. Her breath

190

was death. An unpleasant mixture of marijuana and Listerine.

I stepped back and right off the dock into the icy waters of the lake. When, after the third frozen attempt, I managed to heave my irresistible body back onto the splintery boards of the dock, Helen of Troy and Molokai had rowed back across the Styx. She was nowhere in sight.

41

"WHAT'S the matter, Jack?" Dr. Shimkin said to me later, while I was composing a lovely symphony of birch logs next to the fireplace, ready to be set fire to during the evening and to fill the living room with great puffs of blue-gray fragrances which were guaranteed to kill anyone with incipient emphysema— within seventeen seconds. If the downwind was right, even less time than that. I tried to make myself appear so busy with my nightly chore that I really didn't hear the good doctor.

"Something happen, Jack?" he insisted.

"No," I said, "and you wouldn't believe what didn't happen if I told you."

"What the hell is that supposed to mean?"

Reiko was busy in the kitchen, trying to figure out a new way to serve M & M's. Our two children, Bobby and Timothy, were freely mixing on the floor with Dainty Marie's two yaws carriers. All of them oblivious to the impending black plague. I say "black plague" because I could have been wrong about yaws. Dainty Marie, herself, was sitting in the farthest corner of the room, smoking a Camel and an L & M at the same time. She was far beyond the satisfaction of the old-fashioned, single, one-at-a-time bit. And even two at a time didn't turn her very far on. I'm sure she had an opium pipe stashed away somewhere back in the guest cabin, plus her TWA flight bag full of Mexican alfalfa, but so far she hadn't lit up or cooked up anything in our living room. Not because, I'm sure, she was in the least concerned, but I think that being marooned and far away from her source, she was afraid she might have to share her precious store of go-go goodies.

"I think tonight's the night," I whispered into the good doctor's ear, while acting like I was suddenly interested in his aftershave lotion. (Actually I *was* immensely curious of what he patted onto his face after he'd shaved it. I never had the nerve to ask, but it smelled like Russian leather—taken from an old Russian cavalry horse saddle. It had a manly fragrance, but then again so has a Gary, Indiana, steel puddler.)

"Tonight's the night for *what?*" Dr. Shimkin said, in a voice that could have been heard above a stampede of rabid elephants (on a hot tin roof). Dainty Marie didn't look up from where her navel could have been (if she had one).

"Come into the bedroom," I said to the doctor. Dainty Marie looked quickly up at *this*. She let a Mona Lisa smile tease her thin lips momentarily, then went back to contemplating her midsection.

"What's all the cloak and dagger?" Dr. Shimkin wanted to know.

"All the 'cloak and dagger,'" I said, a little annoyed at the doctor's annoyance, "concerns a certain frozen piece of tail that's about to become defrosted."

"You mean—Marie?" he said.

"No," I said impatiently. "While I was out walking tonight in the woods I just happened to bump into a *moose* who wants to get *laid!*"

"I dunno," the doctor said, deliberating—his face showing great *concern*. I couldn't *believe* it.

"Doctor—" I said, "maybe I should—"

"I dunno," the doctor repeated, "if it's an *old* moose it'll be grateful, but a *young* moose—?"

"Jesus AT&T Christ!" I said. "You *really* got cabin fever! I'm talking about Dainty Marie! I think she's *ready!*"

"For *what?*"

"For *what!*" I was screaming now. "What did you bring her up here for?"

"For a little *fishing*—that's what I *told* her."

"Well, forget the fishing!" I said. "And get her back to your cabin—now! I'll watch her kids. Okay?"

"Oh," the doctor said, "yeah—" He almost slavered. "Yeah—*yeah*—!! I'll get her back to the cabin—right *now!!* I'll tell her the plane is coming and I'll help her pack her knapsack."

"Good," I said. *"Good!"*

I wish I could relate that things worked out just the way the doctor wanted them to, and that he and Dainty Marie had a long-postponed romp in the hay—or at least between the itchy warmth of the Hudson's Bay blankets. But, alas, it was not to be. Dainty Marie had gone back to their cabin believing that they were going back to get ready to leave on a plane that was expected momentarily. And she packed. This didn't take long. When Dr. Shimkin (he told me all about it later) suggested a little farewell gift from *her*, she kicked him in his panting groin.

As Dr. Shimkin lay writhing in superb agony on the cabin floor, Dainty Marie grabbed her things and marched out the door and back to the main lodge.

"So quick?" I said to her.

"How long do you think it takes?" she said.

"Where's Dr. Shimkin?" Reiko wanted to know.

"He's back in the cabin, *resting,*" Marie said.

"Resting *what?*" I said with a merry twinkle in my voice. Dainty Marie didn't answer. She turned her back and started to watch a nonexistent show on a TV set which had been dead for weeks. I thought, as I observed this, maybe she doesn't realize there's *nothing on.* It frightened me. Maybe this was a shadow of things to come. Maybe television stations all over the country would gradually phase out all programs. Then one day there would be no programs left. Every television station would have a full twenty-four hours a day of no programs. There would be nothing on the air at all—and it would all be done so gradually, none of us would ever know. But we'd still sit and stare.

193

42

WHEN next we saw Dr. Shimkin he was walking like Popeye the Sailorman. Or maybe more like James Arness after a four-day horseback ride across the Arizona desert wearing cactus jockey shorts, which I understand is what they make TV cowboys wear to give them that resolute look.

Dr. Shimkin was a terrible sight to behold, but it was the only thing so far at Lost Lake that made Dainty Marie laugh. Her kids and our kids laughed, too. Dr. Shimkin didn't laugh. He didn't smile, either. He was grim clear through, and with every slow step he took he looked like he was biting down on a bullet—the way they used to make soldiers during the Civil War do—during an amputation performed with a dull tree pruner.

"What's up, Doc?" Dainty Marie said, then burst into a fit of what could only be described as derisive hilarity.

"Been jogging, Doc?" Harry Mitchell wanted to know, as Dr. Shimkin shuffled forward without lifting his feet from the floor.

By this time the doctor's agonized slow motion had caught the attention of everyone in the living room. Virgil Palmquist and Reggie Mailer, who had been making plans to *walk* out of the woods—no matter if they died on the way, so long as they were together—studied the doctor's progress with some concern.

"Doctor," Reggie said, "you oughta see a doctor." Then he and Virgil tittered silently. Dr. Shimkin stopped his slow voyage and looked at Virgil and Reggie sitting on the calfskin-covered couch holding hands. He looked from one to the other several times, then he said, his voice an octave higher than it naturally was, "Merle Miller will *never* be President!"

He took another shuffle forward and almost fell prone.

194

Bella Brown was immediately at his side. She grabbed his right arm and lifted him. Abruptly, Dr. Shimkin screamed. This broke up the Frank and Ethel Krasselt and Alice Dotson card game.

"Gee whiz!" Frank Krasselt complained, "I was just about to be the Old Maid." Then to Bella, who had her arms all around the doctor now, holding him erect, "What the hell are you doin', Bella—giving mambo lessons?"

"I'll never mambo again," Dr. Shimkin managed to groan. Dainty Marie laughed. And laughed.

"It's nice that the young people are having fun," Rogers Dotson said, without looking, from the depths of his easy chair in front of the fire, as he tried to find some solace in the miasma of his decomposing meerschaum pipe—dreaming of the bygone days of his Prince Albert-filled canister, all the while stroking with his left hand. He was stroking much higher now, and somehow we had all got the feeling that he had abandoned his nonexistent Irish setter and switched to a nonexistent Shetland pony.

Reiko was unaware of all the drama taking place in the living room. She had spent most of her time in the lodge kitchen trying to concoct palatable dishes from peanut butter, potato chips, flour, and maple syrup. The M & M's were down to three apiece a day—like vitamins. Finally there were no more M & M's—no more potato chips, flour, or maple syrup. All that was left was a two-gallon tin of peanut butter. And nothing to spread it on—unless you had acquired a taste for the palm of your hand. We had to ration the peanut butter to three tablespoons per person per meal, and you had to use your own tablespoon, which *you* were responsible for. I put this rule in effect after I had found out that Sherwood and Elroy, Dainty Marie's two lambkins, had one afternoon, when the rest of us were napping, tossed most of our silverware off the end of the airplane dock into deep water, which I thought was most ironic—even if we'd had a plentiful supply of fancy food, like *escargots*, how the hell would we eat it?

The scarcity of food had become a desperate problem. Everyone, when we had first started to ration things, took it good-naturedly. They all felt, as I did, that any day a passing plane would drop down on Lost Lake and our troubles would be over. This didn't happen, and I was worried. I wish I could say I was worried about our guests. I wasn't. Perverse as it sounds, I was concerned only with Reiko, Bobby, Timothy, and the other members of our family—Wolf, Lady, and their five pups. They were not quite ready to release, and they had to be kept fit for the large ordeal ahead of them. They had to eat, and I was determined to keep my supply of chicken backs, secreted in the ice house, for the wolves only—with an occasional few pieces for Reiko and Bobby and Timothy—which Reiko would make into chicken soup late at night when everyone was asleep in their little cabins—which was about all you could do with chicken backs. I didn't include myself in these sneaky midnight soup orgies because I was terrified that the supply of chicken backs would run out—they were getting mighty low—before I could be sure that the animals would be in tiptop health until I freed them. Also, I wanted to leave them a large cache of food somewhere that they could come back to and feed on if the hunting didn't work too well at first. This might have been a silly idea, because without supervision, I was sure they would not ration this supply well, and other wolves, or almost any other animals except moose and deer, would help themselves. But there was no other way to do it.

The controlled rationing I had imposed on our camp was very unpopular, but eating peanut butter by the spoon, when you are on the verge of starvation is not such a bad idea. Three tablespoons of peanut butter takes more than an eternity to tongue off the roof of your mouth, thus giving your stomach, which is none too bright, the illusion of a prolonged meal.

The peanut butter, washed down with large glasses of ice-cold water which numbed the digestive system, if not too nourishing, at least kept us from thinking deliciously cannibalistic thoughts. Some of the time.

43

THERE were occasional unplanned diversions which kept us from thinking about *ourselves*. Timothy had discovered a bronzed baby shoe which had once been Bobby's when he was Timothy's age. Timothy tried the bronzed shoe on. It fitted him perfectly. We all thought this was very cute, but after clomping around the house all day being cute, when it came time for bed we couldn't get it off.

We tried soap, vaseline, 3-in-1 oil and, finally, prayer. Nothing worked. The lubricants meant nothing, and God didn't know where the hell we were.

What do you do in the middle of nowhere with a baby, three years old, wearing one bronze shoe?

"Maybe we should just leave it on," Harry Mitchell said, surfacing from his martini, "and when we get back to town—buy him another one for his other foot."

"He should have *sneakers,*" Reiko said, practically.

I didn't know what to do. I didn't have the proper cutting tool to cut the bronzed shoe off Timothy's foot, and if I had, there was no way—no room—for a tool to fit inside the shoe for cutting.

"Why don't we sleep on it?" Bella Brown suggested, somewhere around midnight, and that's what we did. The next morning, Bobby's bronzed baby shoe was *off* Timothy's left foot and *on* his right hand. Which was an improvement—we didn't have to listen to that *clomping* all day long.

After the bronzed shoe incident, I started painting again. Every day before I visited the wolves I would put in a couple of hours with my large brush and my large can of red paint. The sides of the cabins didn't need any red paint, so I started painting everything else, whether it needed it or not. I painted the trunks of trees stumps—rocks—bushes—footpaths—puddles—

197

the shoreline—clotheslines—toilet seats—bookcases—books—moose horns—moose droppings—boats—canoes—docks—I tried to corner Sherwood and Erloy but they were wise—they probably had been painted before. I would have painted the air if I'd had a spray gun. I painted and painted and painted—which was sure madness, but it helped me keep my sanity.

On the days when I was so preoccupied with my red paint therapy, Dr. Shimkin would take over my duties with the wolves. This was therapy for him. Driven to the point of frenzy in his daily unrequited capture (he hadn't given up) of Dainty Marie's favors, he needed something, besides what he thought he needed. And he was deadly serious in his study of the wolf.

I had some misgivings in letting him go to Wolf Island alone—not because of any danger of attack but because I didn't think the wolves would show themselves at all. With me he wasn't a stranger, but alone the wolves might consider him just that.

Dr. Shimkin didn't have much luck the first time he went to Wolf Island alone. He didn't see any of *them*. But he felt sure they were watching *him*. About the time of the third visit he brought a chicken back with him and just sat down under a clump of white birch and waited. He had to wait a long time, but finally Wolf, who was actually the more domesticated of any of them, approached him, very cautiously, twitching at the slightest rustle of wind or snapping of a twig. Finally, when Wolf was certain that Dr. Shimkin was the same Dr. Shimkin who had been to Wolf Island with me, he walked over and calmly took the chicken back from Dr. Shimkin's outstretched hand and slowly walked back into the brush.

After an hour or more, Dr. Shimkin told me, Wolf came back. His curiosity, as with all wolves, prompted him to do this. The wolf seems just as fascinated by man as man is by the wolf. Which has proven a very unfortunate trait for the wolf.

What Dr. Shimkin was learning by observing my wolves in this rather false environment I wasn't quite sure, but he was satisfied. And Dr. Shimkin was not the sort who would be quite content to sit home in front of a cosy fire *reading* what others like David Mech, Douglas Pimlott, Stanley Young, or Farley Mowat had to say about wolves. He had to find out for himself, which I thought was admirable, because aside from his youthful study of the wolf, too long a time had passed in between, and Mech, Pimlott, Young, and Mowat had been at it for years, and some of them had started their study of wolves when there were a lot more wolves to study.

"What did you find out about wolves today, Doctor?" I asked him one twilight as he wearily paddled up to the shore. I helped him pull the canoe up out of the darkening water.

"Wolves pee-pee all over the place when they like you," he said.

"You mean Wolf came close enough for you to pet him?"

"He sure did. He wriggled like a puppy and peed, and peed, and PEED!"

"He must be mad about you," I said. "Did he throw himself down on his back and pee right up in the air?"

"Yeah," he said. "Look at me—the first time I decided to wear a white shirt. I never should have scratched his chest."

"He loves that," I said.

"You're telling me—just look at my shirt!" I didn't have to look at his shirt because this used to happen to me. It seemed that no matter how old a wolf gets—I'm speaking of a pet wolf now—they always urinate with pure joy if you show them you care. A puppy habit they never seem to lose.

I was never quite sure of Dr. Shimkin's sincerity in wolf research, although he did put in long hours, because of Dainty Marie—why would a serious scientist bring along a mistress on a scientific expedition? After rereading this last I feel silly. Why *wouldn't* a scientist bring a mistress along on a scientific expedition?

I'll have to ask Jacques Cousteau what the hell *he* does. Sharks can't be all *that* fun!

44

ON the nineteenth day of our trial by peanut butter, I gathered everyone in the living room of the lodge because I had an announcement to make.

"I'm very sorry," I said, looking around the unhappy room, "but from now on the peanut butter has to be rationed." This was greeted by silence. More silence than I have ever heard. No one was even breathing.

"Papa," Bobby said, "nobody likes peanut butter anymore, anyway."

"I know," I said.

"Waddya mean—*rationed?*" Harry Mitchell said in a tone which sounded like he was just one step away from completely reverting to the Cro-Magnon. "All we get now is three tablespoons of peanut butter for each meal!"

"I know," I said, "but from now on you're gonna get just *one* tablespoon—" After the wild screams of protest had died down, I continued, "per day." This brought back the silence. A sinister, bodeful, ominous, black silence. Something was going to happen. Something dreadful, I felt, and I was powerless to stop it. Then something *did* happen—Reiko entered the living room, carrying our pitiful supply of peanut butter in its tin container—and smilingly announced, "soup's on!" A hospitable colloquialism she had picked up from *Bonanza*.

This announcement triggered the revolution. In a split second Reiko had lost the peanut butter tin to a mob. A mob armed with tablespoons. In another few seconds the peanut butter tin was empty. Shiny on the inside as well as the out, and Harry Mitchell, his eyes bloodshot with glory in his triumph over the "system," placed the empty peanut butter tin on the floor and stomped it. Then Virgil Palmquist and Reggie Mailer stomped it. Then Ruthie Mitchell, Rogers and Alice Dotson, Frank and Ethel Krasselt, Bella Brown, Dainty Marie, Sherwood and Elroy—and finally Reiko, Bobby, Timothy, and I stomped it. There was a great satisfaction in this peanut butter tin stomping. It was like an immersion in the Ganges. It washed away our previous troubled lives and left us fresh and clean and ready to begin all over again. It also left us without food.

After this came another long silence, which was the silence of acceptance and not the silence of suppressed revolt, during which we all sat around the living room. No one spoke. None of us looked at each other. Not even the children. They all played separately and quietly. Then they played not at all. They just sat and stared into the future along with everyone else in the black room. The fire had had no fuel ever since the peanut butter tin stomping, and the room was rapidly chilling, but no one made a move toward the wood box.

Hours had passed since this atmosphere of dumb acquiescence had enveloped us like a shroud.

"Have you got a Bible?" Harry Mitchell's sepulchral question startled the whole room.

"I've got the *Soldiers' and Sailors' Prayer Book*," I answered. "It came with the camp."

"We're not soldiers," Rogers Dotson said, from deep in his easy chair, "and we're not sailors. What are we? What are we?" He wasn't really asking a question at all, but Reggie Mailer answered him. "We're stupid!"

"Yes," Virgil Palmquist said. "The Honansville Ecology Group! Out to save the world, and now look at us—starving to death right in the middle of thousands of miles of ecology! To hell with ecology! Let 'em pollute! Let 'em poison the air! Let 'em slaughter the animals! I don't give a good goddamn what they do! From now on, I'm looking out for number one and to hell with everyone else!"

The rest of the Honansville Ecology Group agreed unanimously with Virgil, and in a way I couldn't blame them. The prospect of starvation is not a pleasant one, and it colors our attitude toward everything except, as Virgil had put it, number one. This, I guess, is what is meant by the law of the jungle, the survival of the fittest. The survival of the fittest! This Darwinian rule, as

201

I looked around the living room at our raggle-taggle group, didn't seem to apply at all. We would *all* succumb as *one*. This I was sure of.

That afternoon Charlie Burke set the pontoons of the Canada Goose Airways *Beaver* down onto the ice-flecked waters of Lost Lake and taxied leisurely up to the airplane dock. Charlie Burke greeted us, and I mean *all* of us, who were assembled like it was the beach at Dunkirk on the airplane dock, with such an offhand salutation, as if he had just left us the day before instead of almost three weeks ago.

"How are you folks getting along?" Charlie said, while making the *Beaver* fast to our used-tire-buffered dock. None of us answered. Charlie stopped what he was doing and looked at us once again. Carefully.

"Everything—all right?" he suggested, tentatively. Again there was silence.

"Don't you—*remember* me?" Charlie said—this time concerned. And he might well be. We all stood there like zombies waiting for a new set of batteries. Finally, I said, "Charlie, where have you been? WHERE have you *BEEN?*"

"Well," Charlie said, "yesterday I was up to White Otter Lake—took a buncha moose hunters up there—the moose season ain't for a couple weeks yet, but they wanted to get started on their drinkin'—then the day before that I dropped some stuff off at Marvin the Hermit's cabin on Black Otter Lake, and the day before that—" He took off his checkered woodsman's cap and eased a deer fly from his scalp. "Jesus! Those little bastards bite! The day before that—I'll hafta look at my log book—why?"

"How come you didn't fly over Lost Lake?" Reiko wanted to know.

"Oh, I *did*—yeah—about four days ago—saw your fire —had an outdoor barbecue, huh?"

"Charlie," I said, with very little poise, "that fire was a distress signal! We've been up here for nineteen days without food!" Not an accurate statement but rather dramatic, I thought.

"You all look pretty good," Charlie said. "Need anything from town? Lot of end-of-season sales goin' on down there now."

"All we need from town," Dr. Shimkin said, in a voice edged in black, "is a way to get there! Right now!"

"Oh?" Charlie said. "You all want to go together?" There was a chorus of yesses all done in unison, as if Lenny Bernstein had given the downbeat.

"Well, I dunno," Charlie said. "There's too many of you for one load—if you have any luggage—hafta make two or three trips. Might be dark before I get back." As Charlie was saying this, Dainty Marie and Sherwood and Elroy clambered up the tricky steps of the *Beaver* and grabbed three of the available six seats. Then she motioned to Dr. Shimkin to toss up her knapsack and a few paper bags which she featured as matched luggage. The gesture was so imperial Dr. Shimkin obeyed without question. Then *he* ducked inside the plane's tiny cabin, shouting back to us on the dockside, "Gotta operate in the morning!"

Charlie Burke had to make two more trips to get the Honansville group and their voluminous luggage back to Chinookville and civilization.

"We must do this again next year," Harry Mitchell said, tightly clutching the *Soldiers' and Sailors' Prayer Book* which I had given him. Harry didn't look at me when he said this, and neither did anyone else who was leaving. They didn't speak, either. Harry's seven words were the only ones we heard that acknowledged that they had even been at Lost Lake. Everyone else filed silently up the metal rungs and into the plane. Looking neither to the left nor to the right. Rogers Dotson was the last to clamber aboard the *Beaver*, which he accomplished with some dignity, because he now seemed to be carrying two nonexistent chihuahuas—one under each arm—which made airplane ladder climbing difficult.

As the Canada Goose Airways *Beaver* roared away into the dusk and Reiko and I slowly made our way back to the lodge, with our arms around each other, followed by Bobby holding Timothy's hand for the first time without being told to, we experienced a great wave of relief.

203

We knew Charlie Burke wouldn't be back that eve- ning with the supplies we had ordered, but he had left us some groceries he was supposed to drop off at an- other lake and promised to come back in the morning with everything we needed.

After a delicious meal (of what I couldn't say because after all that peanut butter everything was ambrosia) we sat outside and watched the stars. Again I tried to teach Bobby how to find the North Star and again he struck out. He just couldn't seem to grasp my gentle screamings. Actually I made him so nervous by acting Prussian every time I tried to instruct him in something I felt everyone would know by instinct that I never really taught him anything—except how to duck.

The night was glorious. Black as pitch and cold. I sat there with all I would ever have, *really* have, in my lifetime—my tiny, wonderful family. My little Reiko, with a spirit so pure and kind and full of love. Bobby, grown tall—on the verge of manhood—his face starting to take on the characteristics he would carry for all his life. The slight suggestion of his Oriental ancestry shadowing his eyes. A rough boy. A tough boy, but with the soft heart of his beautiful mother and a deep compassion for all the wild, defenseless creatures of this earth. He sat close to us with his arm around his little brother's shoulders. Timothy was all the bright, precious things of this world combined into one happy, mischievous little boy. Timothy, who at the age of three was so sensitive to his little world and all the things in it that when he saw, for the first time, snow falling, he looked at it for a long, long moment, then he said, quietly, "Indian cry."

As we all sat there, warm, in the sharp chill of the late October night, some of the deep feeling we had had for this remote refuge from the tyrannies of progress began to come back. First, as a trickle—then as a flood. We loved this great wilderness which surrounded us.

From far off, we heard the mournful, but beautiful, howl of a wolf. Then we heard the howls of a full wolf pack. Maybe they were ours. We had no way of knowng, but the sound heightened the feeling of being in a aallowed place. This great, virgin forest. This vast, untouched land. This shining country. This Canada. It *is* aallowed.

45

NOT long after the overdue departure of our unhappy guests was the date we had set to release Wolf, Lady, and the pups, Dancer, Prancer, Dunder, Blitzen, and Wolfie into the big woods, and as the time grew short I was on the verge once again of abandoning the whole idea and getting them back to the safety of their pen in Honansville. But every time I went over to feed them on the island and saw how happy and completely contented they seemed, I knew I could never lock them up again. Even the memory of the undesirable visit of The Hunter a couple of months back did not deter me. They *must* be free.

November 1, the day we had chosen to take the wolves off the too-confining island—which looked much smaller now that the wolves were much bigger. Even Wolf and Lady seemed to have grown and filled out during their stay there, and the pups now looked like full-grown wolves, although they were just a little more than six months old.

November 1 was a cold, blustery day, with the threat of snow constantly showing in the fast-moving gray-black clouds scudding across the oppressive sky.

We caged and moved the pups first, across the half mile or so of the still open water of the lake, and released them on a long neck of pine-covered land that fingered out from the west bank. The pups immediately started sniffing out the territory, as wolves do—not missing a thing in their effort to either assure themselves there was no danger or to look for field mice. They seemed to stay fairly well bunched, and I really couldn't tell which was which among them, except that the females were smaller.

After all the pups were safely ashore on the mainland peninsula, we went back to the island for Wolf and Lady. Getting *them* into the transporting cages was another matter entirely. The pups had been still a little naïve when it came to cages, and although it was a mighty struggle, we had managed it; but Wolf and Lady could not be enticed to come anywhere *near* the cages.

We tried putting a rope on Lady and dragging her into the cage opening from the back of the cage. But she struggled so, and I was afraid that what had happened to my beloved Tanuki, who died while resisting this same sort of thing, might happen again. It made me stop and reconsider. We *couldn't* leave the pups on the mainland overnight by themselves, so we had to figure out something.

"Can wolves swim?" Bobby asked. Why hadn't *I* thought of this? Of course they can swim—any animal can. So it looked like Wolf and Lady were going to have to swim to join their offspring—something they might have done on their own, anyway, but we couldn't be sure and I didn't want to take the chance.

First we put long ropes around Wolf's and Lady's necks. Wolf didn't seem to mind because he had been walked daily on a leash for a couple of years; but Lady thought we were going to pull the same stunt again with the cage, and she gave us a lot of trouble—dashing into the brush whenever I approached her with the looped rope or just running off a little where I couldn't reach her. Finally she forgot about the cage routine and started to treat the whole thing as a game. She circled Reiko and Bobby, Timothy and me—getting closer and closer, but not close enough. I tried to lasso her but caught nothing but rocks and bushes. Finally I gave Bobby the rope and approached Lady without it. Immediately she came to me and accepted a dog biscuit. Then I started to rub her spine and talk baby talk to her. She responded just as Wolf always did. She turned her body into a U-shape and wriggled and crouched and looked tickled as all hell. She loved this treatment.

ll the while, I moved closer to Bobby, and just at the right moment, when Lady was at the height of her ecstasy, Bobby dropped the loop of the rope over her head and she was caught.

Now all we had to do was get the boat started and the two wolves into the water and swimming. We knew we couldn't just pull them into the water unceremoniously—it would be the cage resistance thing again. So we let them run around with the ropes on their necks while we had some sandwiches and coffee. After an hour or so Wolf and Lady forgot that they were wearing ropes, and we invited them out on the big rock, which we used as a landing for the island, and gave them bits of goodies. At the same time, Bobby was in the boat at the "ready" when we gave the signal. Finally, after Wolf and Lady had both been lulled into a lovely false sense of security with cookies, candy, and a beef knuckle each, Reiko and I moved into the boat like thieves in the night, while Wolf and Lady were gnawing contentedly and unknowingly at their huge beef bones. At a nod from me Bobby started the outboard motor (and thank God it started on the first pull of the starting cord), and Wolf and Lady found themselves yanked off the rock and into the water—swimming. Lady had lost her bone in the surprise move, but Wolf instinctively hung onto his, which made him choke because the water had gotten into his jammed-open mouth.

Neither Wolf, who soon abandoned his beef bone, nor Lady could resist too strenuously the pull of the boat on their ropes, so they had no choice but to follow us, swimming strongly. This surprise move caught Timothy unawares, too. We had to leave him crying his heart out on the island. Orphaned, he must have thought at the moment, by the most cruel and callous parents in the whole world. He screamed for us to come back, but we were towing two wolves and just couldn't make it.

The half-mile swim to the mainland peninsula and the wolf pups didn't take very long. The wolves were very powerful swimmers, and after the first few moments of what amounted almost to embarrassment, having been caught off guard, they seemed to enjoy it. Lady reached

207

over a few times on the way and nipped at Wolf, and he nipped back.

When we crunched into the shore of the peninsula the five wolf pups had stopped all their sniffing and investigating and were standing, waiting for us. I quickly, but not enthusiastically, jumped out of the boat into the icy water and slipped the ropes off Wolf and Lady just before their feet touched bottom—it was easier this way —and as soon as they were free of the water, they shook themselves and showered all of us, and their pups too.

The pups wriggled themselves silly at being reunited with Wolf and Lady. They dashed all around them, licking and nuzzling them and acting like they were never so glad to see anyone in their whole lives, and this was probably true. They were still very dependent on their parents—especially on Wolf. He would have to be the big provider now.

We stayed for a few more minutes while this display of filial devotion was taking place. Wolf and Lady responded with little nips of warm affection for their happy brood. It was a grand reunion, but we knew it was now or never. We had to leave. I had to steel myself to keep from revealing the turmoil that raged within me as I shoved the boat away from the shore.

All of the pups, Dancer, Prancer, Dunder, Blitzen, and Wolfie—how ridiculous before, but how sweet these names sounded now—seemed surprised. So did Wolf and Lady. As we pulled farther and farther out into the lake, snow started to fall softly, silently. The wolves were now on a slight, rocky promontory, watching us disappear into the white haze. Wolf stood in front, his two enormous forepaws on a fallen log. Lady slightly back, but by his side. The five pups formed a semicircle behind them. It was a lovely picture and one I will *never* forget. They all looked so beautiful and strong—and yet in the gathering darkness of the November day, so pathetically alone and defenseless.